THE *Lost Tools* OF WRITING

LEVEL ONE
STUDENT WORKBOOK

PUBLISHED BY

 CiRCE INSTITUTE
CULTIVATING WISDOM & VIRTUE

The CiRCE Institute is a non-profit 501(c)3 organization that exists to promote and support classical education in the school and in the home. We identify the ancient principles of learning, communicate them enthusiastically, and apply them vigorously in today's educational settings through curricula development, teacher training, events, an online academy, and a content-laden website.

CIRCE INSTITUTE
81 McCachern Blvd, Concord, NC, 28025
704.795.7944 | info@circeinstitute.org | www.circeinstitute.org

PERMISSIONS

Teachers who purchase or for whom schools purchase the complete *The Lost Tools of Writing*™ package are granted permission to duplicate pages from the Teacher's Guide for their personal use. They are also granted permission to copy pages from the Teacher's Guide as reference pages for their students, including, but not limited to, the assessment guides provided in this Teacher's Guide.

One Student Workbook should be purchased for each student who is taught *The Lost Tools of Writing*™. Some Invention worksheets will be imitated more than once. If the teacher or student wishes to copy these pages, they may do so, but only for the individual student who possesses the Student Workbook. Students are also encouraged to imitate the pattern of the worksheet on their own paper.

Permission is not granted to copy worksheets or exercise forms or any other material from one student's workbook for other students.

Permission is granted for quotations and short excerpts to be used in published materials with the condition that the source of those quotations and excerpts is included in the published materials.

For longer excerpts, please contact us at www.circeinstitute.org.

ACKNOWLEDGEMENTS

The Lost Tools of Writing is the product of a vast team effort.

Thousands of teachers and students have experienced *The Lost Tools of Writing*™, and many have been generous with their suggestions and feedback. This fifth edition is our enthusiastic "Thank You!!" to everyone who helped us make *The Lost Tools of Writing*™ the best composition program in the world.

The authors of this Fifth Edition are Leah Lutz and Andrew Kern, with contributions from Camille Goldston, Renee Mathis, David Kern, and Arlene Roemer da Feltre.

Special acknowledgement is due to the members and alumni of the CiRCE Institute Apprenticeship, who have taught, practiced, reviewed, and developed *The Lost Tools of Writing*™ in their various contexts.

Furthermore, thank you to all who have participated in a *Lost Tools Of Writing*™ Workshop, to teachers who have been part of an in-house *Lost Tools Of Writing*™ Teacher Training, to parents who stole a Saturday from their busy schedules, and to heads of school who demonstrated their commitment to classical education when they supported their teachers' efforts to achieve excellence in both classical composition and classical teaching.

The CiRCE Institute is a not-for-profit corporation, dependent upon and grateful for the generosity of benefactors who share her vision for classical education. If not for the tremendous support of so many fellow believers, *The Lost Tools of Writing*™ would never have seen the light of day. You have sustained us, and it would be wrong to fail to acknowledge and thank you.

TABLE *of* CONTENTS

TABLE *of* CONTENTS

ESSAY
ONE

Essay One Invention
THE ANI CHART

Write your Issue.

_____

Fill out the form below.

AFFIRMATIVE (A)	NEGATIVE (N)	INTERESTING (I)

Essay One Arrangement
FROM ANI TO OUTLINE

Write your Issue.

_____

Thesis & Proof

Use the information you generated during the Invention process to decide whether you will craft the Affirmative or Negative argument.

☐ *Affirmative*

☐ *Negative*

Rewrite the issue as a Thesis statement.

_____

Write the first reason (Proof 1) for your Thesis.

_____

_____

Write the second reason (Proof 2) for your Thesis.

_____

_____

Write the third reason (Proof 3) for your Thesis.

_____

_____

Conclusion
Summarize your argument

Repeat the Thesis.

_____

Repeat the main Proofs.

_____

_____

_____

Introduction
Introduce your argument

Write your Thesis.

_____

Add the Enumeration (the number of Proofs).

_____

List your three Proofs.

_____

_____

_____

5

Arrangement Template One
RUDIMENTARY PERSUASIVE OUTLINE

Transcribe your outline onto a separate page, imitating the template provided below. Do not use complete sentences.

Replace lines that have an asterisk with your information from the Arrangement Worksheet on the previous pages.

I. Introduction
    A. Thesis*

    B. Enumeration*

    C. Exposition
        1. Proof I*
        2. Proof II*
        3. Proof III*

II. Proof
    A. Proof 1*

    B. Proof 2*

    C. Proof 3*

III. Conclusion
    A. Thesis*

    B. Summary of Proof
        1. Proof I*
        2. Proof II*
        3. Proof III*

ESSAY TWO

Essay Two Invention

INTRODUCTION TO THE FIVE TOPICS

*The following questions introduce the **Five Common Topics of Invention** that you use whenever you make decisions. You will learn much more about each topic in later lessons. Answers to these questions can be placed in your I column on the ANI chart.*

Comparison Questions

- *How is X similar to Y?*
- *How is X different from Y?*

Definition Questions

- *Who or what is X?*
- *What kind of thing is X?*

Circumstance Questions

- *What was happening in the same place and time as your issue or situation?*
- *What was happening at the same time as, but in different places from, your issue or situation?*

Relation Questions

- *What led to the situation in which a decision needs to be made?*
- *What followed the decision?*

Testimony Questions

- *What do witnesses say about the character or his actions?*

Review your I column, and move any appropriate
items to the A or N columns.

Essay Two Arrangement
A GUIDE TO SORTING

Step One

Sort the items in the A column into groups as follows:

Sort into Group 1

- Place a symbol (such as @ or $) by the first item in the A column.

- Look at the second item in the column, and determine whether it can be placed in the same group as the first item. If it can, place the same symbol next to the second item.

- Review the list, and determine whether each item can be placed in the same group as the first. Mark these with the same symbol.

Sort into Group 2

- Return to the second item in the list, and place a different symbol by it.

- Look at each remaining item in the list to determine whether it can be placed in the same group as the second item. Place the symbol you used for the second item beside each succeeding item that can be included in the same group as the second item.

Keep sorting into new groups

- Review the entire list, placing a new symbol by any item that could be the first member of a new group. Add additional items to each new group. Your goal is to form five groups of related items, all clearly marked with symbols.

- Name each group with a fitting heading or summary phrase.

List these group names below:

1.

2.

3.

4.

5.

Circle the three most compelling groups.

Step Two

Sort the items in the N column as you did in the A column.

- Sort the items into groups with new symbols.

- Name each group with a fitting heading or summary phrase.

List these group names below:

1.

2.

3.

4.

5.

Circle the three most compelling groups.

Step Three

Decide whether you will defend the A or N argument.

Write the Thesis you will defend:

_____

_____

From the side you have chosen to defend, write the group names you circled above. These groups are your Proofs to defend your Thesis.

_____

_____

From the sorting you completed above, list three Sub-Proofs (the members of each group you made) for each Proof:

1a. _____

1b. _____

1c. _____

2a. _____

2b. _____

2c. _____

3a. _____

3b. _____

3c. _____

Essay Two Arrangement B

INTRODUCTORY PERSUASIVE ESSAY WORKSHEET

Write your Issue.

_____

Thesis & Proof

Rewrite your issue as a Thesis statement.

_____

Write the first Proof for your Thesis.

_____

List three Sub-Proofs that support your first Proof.

_____

_____

_____

Write the second Proof for your Thesis.

_____

List three Sub-Proofs that support your second Proof.

_____

_____

_____

Write the third Proof for your Thesis.

_____

List three Sub-Proofs that support your third Proof.

Conclusion
Summarize your argument.

Repeat the Thesis.

Repeat the main Proofs.

Introduction
Introduce your argument.

Write your Thesis.

Add the Enumeration.

List your three main Proofs.

Essay Two Arrangement Template
INTRODUCTORY PERSUASIVE ESSAY

Transcribe your outline onto a separate page, using the template provided below. Do not use complete sentences.

Replace lines that have an asterisk with your information from the Arrangement Worksheet on the previous pages.

I. Introduction
      A. Thesis*

      B. Enumeration*

      C. Exposition
             1. Proof I*
             2. Proof II*
             3. Proof III*

II. Proof
      A. Proof I*
             1. Sub-Proof 1*
             2. Sub-Proof 2*
             3. Sub-Proof 3*
      B. Proof II*
             1. Sub-Proof 1*
             2. Sub-Proof 2*
             3. Sub-Proof 3*
      C. Proof III*
             1. Sub-Proof 1*
             2. Sub-Proof 2*
             3. Sub-Proof 3*

III. Conclusion
      A. Thesis*

      B. Summary of Proof
             1. Proof I*
             2. Proof II*
             3. Proof III*

Essay Two Elocution
PARALLELISM I: WORDS

Definition

Parallelism is similarity of structure in a pair or series
of related words, phrases, or clauses (sentences).

Review
List the parts of speech, and provide two or three examples of each.

_____

_____

_____

_____

_____

_____

_____

_____

_____

_____

_____

Steps to Using Parallelism

1. Find a term in your writing that you can expand by adding detail: *Edmund.*

2. Generate a list of words in the same part of speech as this term: *Lucy.*
    Or list words that relate to your term. List these words by part of speech*: verb-heed, adjective-spoiled, adverb-quickly.*

3. Select one series of words that are the same part of speech, and add this parallel list to a sentence in your essay. Rewrite the sentence as needed to express a clear, complete thought: *Edmund should heed, follow, and obey the White Witch.*

Examples

From J. R. R. Tolkien's *The Hobbit*

"Not a *nasty, dirty, wet* hole, filled with the ends of
worms and an oozy smell . . ."

From J. R. R. Tolkien's *The Hobbit*

". . . not yet a *dry, bare, sandy* hole with nothing in
it to sit down on or to eat: it was a hobbit hole, and
that means comfort."

From Earnest Hemingway's *A Farewell to Arms*

"What a beautiful bridge, Aymo said. It was a *long plain iron*
bridge across what was usually a dry river-bed."

EXAMPLE

Term
Edmund

Nouns
Lucy, Susan, Peter

Parallel Structure
Edmund, Lucy, Susan, and Peter are siblings.

Verb
Heed, follow, obey

Parallel Structure
Edmund should heed, follow, and obey the White Witch.

Adjectives
Spoiled, angry, jealous

Parallel Structure
The spoiled, jealous, angry Edmund considered the
White Witches offer.

Adverb
Quickly, willingly, foolishly

Parallel Structure
Edmund followed the Witch quickly, willingly, and foolishly.

Practice

1. List two terms from your ~~issue~~ essay.

_____

_____

Move these terms to the chart below.

2. List parts of speech for each term using the corresponding boxes in the chart.

PART OF SPEECH	TERM A_____	TERM B_____
Nouns (list nouns related to your term):		
Verbs (list actions related to your term):		
Adjectives (list adjectives related to the term):		
Adverbs (list adverbs related to a verb or adjective above):		

3. Use two or three words from one list to create sentences with parallel word structure. Be sure to check your sentence construction. Parallel lists need proper punctuation and conjunctions.

_____

_____

_____

TIPS

Pairs will be joined with a conjunction.

A series is a group of three or more elements in a row.
The last element in the series is usually connected to the others
with one of these coordinating conjunctions: *and, or, but (not), or*
yet (not).

Commas should be placed between each element in the series, and before the
coordinating conjunction.

Now add your own examples of parallelism to Essay Two.

ESSAY THREE

Essay Three Invention
COMPARISON I: SIMILARITIES

List the two terms you will compare.

A_____   B_____

WHAT DO BOTH HAVE?	WHAT ARE BOTH?	WHAT DO BOTH DO?

Review your I column and move any
appropriate items to the A or N columns.

Essay Three Arrangement A
A GUIDE TO EXORDIUM

Use each of the following kinds of Exordium to generate possible openings for your essay.

Ask three questions.

_____

_____

_____

Write two things you can challenge your readers to do.

_____

_____

Provide a quotation relevant to the issue.

Source:

_____

_____

Quotation:

_____

_____

_____

_____

_____

_____

_____

_____

Essay Three Arrangement B

BASIC PERSUASIVE ESSAY WITH EXORDIUM

Write your ~~Thesis statement~~ *issue*.

_____

Thesis & Proof

Review your Invention, and decide whether you will support the Affirmative or Negative case. Rewrite the Issue as a Thesis statement.

_____

Write the first Proof for your Thesis.

_____

List three Sub-Proofs that support your first Proof.

_____

_____

_____

Write the second Proof for your Thesis.

_____

List three Sub-Proofs that support your second Proof.

_____

_____

_____

Write the third Proof for your Thesis.

_____

List three Sub-Proofs that support your third Proof.

_____

_____

_____

Conclusion
Summarize your argument

Repeat the Thesis.

_____

Repeat the main Proofs.

_____

_____

_____

_____

Introduction
Introduce your argument

Write your Thesis.

_____

Add the Enumeration.

_____

List your three main Proofs.

_____

_____

_____

Choose and add an Exordium.

_____

_____

_____

_____

Essay Three Arrangement Template
BASIC PERSUASIVE ESSAY

Transcribe your outline onto a separate page, imitating the template provided below. Do not use complete sentences.

Replace lines that have an asterisk with *your* information from the Arrangement Worksheet on the previous pages.

I. Introduction

    A. *Exordium* *
    B. *Thesis**
    C. *Enumeration**
    D. *Exposition*
        1. Proof I*
        2. Proof II*
        3. Proof III*

II. Proof
    A. *Proof I**
        1. Sub-Proof 1*
        2. Sub-Proof 2*
        3. Sub-Proof 3*
    B. *Proof II**
        1. Sub-Proof 1*
        2. Sub-Proof 2*
        3. Sub-Proof 3*
    C. *Proof III**
        1. Sub-Proof 1*
        2. Sub-Proof 2*
        3. Sub-Proof 3*

III. Conclusion
    A. *Thesis**

    B. *Summary of Proof*
        1. Proof I*
        2. Proof II*
        3. Proof III*

Essay Three Elocution

BASIC EDITING: VERBS

What is a verb?

_____

_____

Examples of Active and Precise Verbs

❖ From Herman Melville's *Moby Dick*

*"Such a portentous and mysterious monster **roused** all my curiosity."*

❖ From Genesis 2:7

*"And the LORD God **formed** man of the dust of the ground, and **breathed** into his nostrils the breath of life; and man became a living soul."*

❖ From John Magee's "High Flight"

*"Oh! I have **slipped** the surly bonds of Earth*
*And **danced** the skies on laughter-silvered wings ..."*

Building Stronger Sentences

Step #1: Use Precise Verbs

Conversational patterns are often wordy and imprecise when used in writing.

Consider the following sentences:

1. *He got a gift from Father Christmas.*
2. *She got a glimpse of the faun.*
3. *They had a chance to sail home.*

4. *He has shiny armor.*
5. *The wolf went out in search of the children and beavers.*
6. *The children went for a walk through the new house.*

Rewrite each sentence above, replacing each *have/had/has*, *go/went*, and *get/got* with an action verb. Communicate the action with more precision.

1. _____

2. _____

3. _____

4. _____

5. _____

6. _____

Step #2: Use Active Verbs

A passive verb hides the actor of a sentence.

Consider the following sentences:
1. *The sleigh was being driven fast.*
2. *Mrs. Jones' floor was cleaned by her daughter.*
3. *In the tent, the armor was left abandoned by Achilles.*
4. *During Narnian winter, the fauns were turned to stone by the White Witch.*
5. *The wardrobe was entered separately.*
6. *The wine-dark sea was navigated skillfully.*

Rewrite each sentence above with a more active verb.

1. _____

2. _____

3. _____

4. _____

5. _____

6. _____

Practice

Generate your own sentences:

1. List three subjects.

_____

_____

_____

2. With those subjects, write sentences with precise, active verbs.

_____

_____

_____

_____

_____

_____

_____

Essay Application

Check your current essay for vague and passive verbs.
Correct those sentences as necessary.

ESSAY FOUR

Essay Four Invention

COMPARISON II: DIFFERENCES

List the two terms you will compare.

A_____   B_____

	A does more/less_____ Verb than B (describe the difference).	A does _____ Verb better/worse than B (describe the difference).
BOTH A & B DO (LIST VERBS)		
BOTH A & B HAVE (LIST NOUNS BOTH HAVE)	A has more/less _____ Noun than B (describe the difference).	A has better/worse _____ Noun than B (describe the difference).
BOTH A & B ARE (LIST ADJECTIVES BOTH SHARE)	A is more_____ than B. Describe Adjective Difference	
BOTH A & B ARE (LIST GROUPS BOTH BELONG TO)		A is better/worse_____ Group Member than B (describe the difference):

Identify one different group to which each term belongs and use those groups to complete the following sentence.

Examples:

While Edmund is a human boy, the White Witch is a native of Charn. While an

apple is a pomme fruit, an orange is a citrus fruit.

While Achilles is a Greek, Hector is a Trojan.

While_____(Term A) is

_____(a group or kind of thing),

_____(Term B) is

_____(a different
group or kind of thing).

**Review your I column, and move any
appropriate items to the A or N columns.**

Essay Four Arrangement A

BASIC PERSUASIVE ESSAY
WITH AMPLIFICATION

Write your Thesis statement.

_____

Identify your audience.

_____

Select the person or groups the audience cares about, and explain how the group
will be affected by this issue.

- o   Animals or an animal

   _____

- o   Family or family members

   _____

- o   Friends of your audience

   _____

- o   Ancestors

   _____

- o   Descendants

   _____

- o   A specific group of people (identify)

   _____

- o   Local community

   _____

o   Community leaders

_____

o   Government (local, state, national)

_____

o   Voluntary Organizations (e.g. Church, Boy Scouts)

_____

o   God

_____

o   Other

_____

Choose the one thing, person, or group on whom your Thesis would have the most impact.

o   To whom your Thesis matters

_____

o   Why does your Thesis matter to them?

_____

Essay Four Arrangement B

BASIC PERSUASIVE ESSAY WITH AMPLIFICATION

Write your Issue.

_____

Thesis & Proof

Review your Invention, and decide whether you will support the Affirmative or Negative case. Rewrite the issue as a Thesis statement.

_____

Write the first Proof for your Thesis.

_____

List three Sub-Proofs that support your first Proof.

_____

_____

_____

Write the second Proof for your Thesis.

_____

List three Sub-Proofs that support your second Proof.

_____

_____

_____

Write the third Proof for your Thesis.

_____

List three Sub-Proofs that support your third reason.

_____

_____

_____

Conclusion
Summarize your argument

Repeat your Thesis.

_____

Repeat the main Proofs.

_____

_____

_____

Amplification

Outline an Amplification, showing to whom your Thesis matters and why.

It matters to _____ ,

because _____

Introduction

Introduce your argument

Write your Thesis.

_____

Add the Enumeration.

_____

List your three main Proofs.

_____

_____

_____

Choose and add an Exordium.

_____

_____

_____

_____

Essay Four Arrangement Template
BASIC PERSUASIVE ESSAY

Transcribe your outline onto a separate page, using the template provided below. Do not use complete sentences.

Replace lines that have an asterisk with *your* information from the Arrangement Worksheet on the previous pages.

I. Introduction
    A. Exordium*
    B. Thesis*
    C. Enumeration*
    D. Exposition*
        1. Proof I*
        2. Proof II*
        3. Proof III*

II. Proof
    A. Proof I*
        1. Sub-Proof 1*
        2. Sub-Proof 2*
        3. Sub-Proof 3*
    B. Proof II*
        1. Sub-Proof 1*
        2. Sub-Proof 2*
        3. Sub-Proof 3*
    C. Proof III*
        1. Sub-Proof 1*
        2. Sub-Proof 2*
        3. Sub-Proof 3*

III. Conclusion
    A. Thesis*
    B. Summary of Proof
        1. Proof I*
        2. Proof II*
        3. Proof III*
    C. Amplification
        1. To whom it matters*
        2. Why it matters to that person or group*

Essay Four Elocution

PARALLELISM II: PHRASES & CLAUSES

Definition

Parallelism is similarity of structure in a pair or series of related words, phrases, or clauses (sentences).

Review

1. List the parts of speech.

_____

2. What is a phrase?

_____

3. Give two examples of a phrase.

_____

_____

4. What is a clause?

_____

5. Give two examples of clauses.

_____

_____

Examples

Words can be parallel, as in the following:

From Shakespeare's *The Tragedy of Julius Caesar*

"*Friends, Romans, Countrymen*, lend me your ears;
I come to bury Caesar, not to praise him."

From Washington Irving's "Rip Van Winkle"

"*Morning, noon, and night*, her tongue was incessantly going, and everything
he said or did was sure to produce a torrent of household eloquence."

From Homer's *Iliad*

"...the shaker of the earth did not fail to hear the goddess, *but came* up among them
from the sea, *and sat* in the midst of them, *and asked* Zeus of his counsel."
XX, 13-15

Phrases can be parallel, as in the following:

From the *Ad Herrenium*

"The Romans *destroyed Numantia, razed Carthage,
obliterated Corinth, overthrew Fregellae*."

From Washington Irving's "Rip Van Winkle"

"Here they used to sit in the shade through a long lazy summer's day, *talking listlessly over village gossip, or telling endless sleepy stories about nothing.*"

Clauses can be parallel, as in the following:

Plutarch's Life 8

From Julius Caesar

"I came; I saw; I conquered."

From Charles Dickens's *Great Expectations*

"A boy may lock his door, *[he] may be warm in bed, [he] may tuck himself up, [he] may draw the clothes over his head, [he] may think himself comfortable and safe,* but that young man will softly creep and creep his way to him and tear him open."

Student Examples

The Nightingale should have returned to sing for the Emperor for three reasons: she brought him comfort, she saved him from Death, and she changed the Emperor to a better man.

Odysseus debated whether to pull out his sword, throw down his shield, and cut off his head.

> Socrates and Phaedrus should walk to the tall plane tree for three reasons: the walk will benefit their bodies, their minds, and their souls.

> Aeneas's identity demands his action, his action magnifies his reputation, and his reputation opens his future.

Steps to using parallelism in your sentence structure:

Either find a phrase or clause in your writing that you can expand by adding detail or use parallel structure to rewrite sentences you have already written. Your three Proofs are a great place to start.

If you want to add to a sentence:

    a.   Identify a sentence with a phrase or clause that contains a structure that can be imitated. Some things to look for: prepositional phrases, infinitives, noun phrases, or adjective/adverb clauses, e.g.. *"in the beginning"*.

    b. Generate additional phrases or clauses that follow the same structure as the one you chose above, e.g., *"at the midpoint", "after the end"*.

    c.   Select two phrases or clauses to add to the one you chose in step a.

    d.   Expand your sentence, adding the two new phrases or clauses and following the same pattern as the first. Make any other changes necessary to keep the sentence coherent.

If you want to rewrite existing clauses or phrases (such as your Proofs):

    a.   Choose a phrase or clause that follows a pattern that later phrases or clauses could imitate (for the sake of this exercise, treat a sentence like a clause). The first proof can be very useful for this exercise because you know there will be a series of clauses that follows the same pattern.

    b. Identify the pattern followed by your chosen phrase or clause.

    c.   Find two other phrases or clauses that are related to the one you chose above.

    d. Compare their patterns to determine whether they can be made parallel to the first. Would their relationship to the first be clearer if they were made parallel?

    e.   Try several different ways to make them parallel until you find the pattern that works best.

Practice

1. Add more details to a sentence.

   A. Pick a phrase or clause from your writing.

   _____

   _____

   B. Generate several additional phrases or clauses

   _____

   _____

2. Rewrite a sentence or several sentences with parallel structure.

   _____

   _____

   _____

TIPS

Remember to keep writing in parallel structure.
Keep an eye on those **parts of speech**!

Be sure to **check** your sentence construction.
Parallel **lists** need proper punctuation and conjunctions.

Pairs will be joined with a **conjunction.**

A **series** is a group of three or more elements in a row.
The last element in the series is commonly connected
to the others with one of these coordinating
conjunctions:
and, or, but (not), or yet (not).

Commas should be placed between each element in the series
and before the coordinating conjunction.

**Now add your own examples of
parallelism to Essay Four.**

ESSAY FIVE

Essay Five Invention
DEFINITION I

1. Identify a term from your issue.

_____

2. List three or four groups this term belongs to.

_____

3. Select a group from the list above which will be helpful for you as you define the term.

_____

4. List other members (three or four) of the group you selected.

_____

_____

_____

_____

5. Identify a common characteristic of all members of this group (What quality do all the members share?).

_____

_____

_____

_____

6. What characteristic makes the term _different from these other group members?_

_____

7. **Write your definition.** Include the term, its group, and its difference. In other words, state that the term is a member of its group and how it is different from all the other members.

EXAMPLES

Term: blue whale
Group: mammal
Difference: largest known to have existed
Definition: The blue whale is the largest mammal known to exist.

Term: Mr. Tumnus
Group: faun
Difference: invited Lucy to tea
Definition: Mr. Tumnus is a faun who invited Lucy to tea

Your Definition:

_____

_____

_____

**Review your I column, and move any
appropriate items to the A or N columns.**

Essay Five Arrangement
DIVISION

Write your Thesis.

_____

Write your Counter-Thesis.

_____

Common Opinions

Regarding your issue, *it is commonly agreed that...*

_____
_____
_____
_____
_____
_____
_____

Is there anything that both sides want, fear, or believe?

_____
_____

Agreement

On what do both sides agree?

_____

_____

_____

_____

_____

Choose one point of agreement.

_____

_____

_____

Disagreement

Some people believe (Thesis):

_____

_____

Conversely, some other people believe (Counter-Thesis):

_____

_____

Essay Five Arrangement B

BASIC PERSUASIVE ESSAY WITH DIVISION

Write your issue.

_____

Thesis & Proof

Review your Invention and decide whether you will support the affirmative or negative case. Rewrite the issue as a Thesis statement.

_____

Write the first Proof for your Thesis.

_____

List three Sub-Proofs that support your first Proof.

_____

_____

_____

Write the second Proof for your Thesis.

_____

List three Sub-Proofs that support your second Proof.

_____

_____

_____

Write the third Proof for your Thesis.

_____

List three Sub-Proofs that support your third proof.

_____

_____

_____

Conclusion
Summarize your argument

Repeat your Thesis.

_____

Repeat the main Proofs.

_____

_____

_____

Amplification

Outline an Amplification, showing to whom your **Thesis statement matters** and why.

It matters to _____

because _____

Division
Clarifying the Argument

State the agreement between you and your opponent.

_____

_____

_____

State the two positions that can be taken.

Affirmative position

_____

Negative position

_____

Distribution

Write your Thesis.

_____

Add the Enumeration.

_____

List your main Proofs.

_____

_____

_____

Introduction
Introduce your argument

Choose and add an Exordium.

_____

_____

_____

_____

Essay Five Arrangement Template
BASIC PERSUASIVE ESSAY

Transcribe your outline onto a separate page, using the template provided below. Do not use complete sentences.

Replace lines that have an asterisk with *your* information from the Arrangement Worksheet on the previous pages.

I. Introduction
    A. Exordium*
    B. Division
        1. Agreement*
        2. Disagreement
            a. Thesis*
            b. Counter-Thesis*
    C. Distribution
        1. Thesis*
        2. Enumeration*
        3. Exposition*
            a. Proof I*
            b. Proof II*
            c. Proof III*

II. Proof
    A. Proof I*
        1. Sub-Proof 1*
        2. Sub-Proof 2*
        3. Sub-Proof 3*
    B. Proof II*
        1. Sub-Proof 1*
        2. Sub-Proof 2*
        3. Sub-Proof 3*
    C. Proof III*
        1. Sub-Proof 1*
        2. Sub-Proof 2*
        3. Sub-Proof 3*

III. Conclusion
    A. Thesis*
    B. Summary of Proof
        3. Proof I*
        4. Proof II*
        5. Proof III*
    C. Amplification
        6. To whom it matters*
        7. Why it matters to that person or group*

 Essay Five Elocution

ANTITHESIS

Definition

Antithesis is a scheme in which strongly contrasting
(or opposite) ideas are expressed in parallel form.

Examples

From Neil Armstrong's Moon Landing Speech

"That's one **small step for man**; one **giant leap for mankind."**

From Alexander Pope's *An Essay on Criticism*

"To err is human; to forgive divine."

From Martin Luther King, Jr.'s *I Have a Dream* Speech

"I have a dream that my four little children will one day live in a nation where they will
not be judged **by the color of their skin** but **by the content of their character**.
I have a *dream* today!"

> **From Charles Dicken's *A Tale of Two Cities***
>
> "It was the **best** of times, it was the **worst** of times, it was the age of **wisdom**, it was the age of **foolishness**, it was the epoch of **belief**, it was the epoch of **incredulity**, it was the season of **Light**, it was the season of **Darkness**, it was **the spring of hope**, it was **the winter of despair**, we had **everything** before us, we had **nothing** before us, we were all going direct to **Heaven**, we were all going direct **the other way**."

Steps to Creating Antithesis

1. Find an idea in your writing for which you can create a contrasting phrase or clause. *Edmund should not follow the White Witch.*
2. Generate a contrasting phrase or clause. *He should follow Lucy.*
3. Make the second idea parallel to the first and rewrite your sentence using these two contrasting ideas in parallel form. *Edmund should not follow the White Witch. However, he should follow Lucy.*

Student Examples

> Edmund was a confused, lost boy, while the White Witch was a conniving, plotting ruler.

> Edmund hoped for power, but settled for promises.

> Though Odysseus accomplished his own homecoming, his crew lost their lives.

> He lived in weakness but died in strength.

> The sacrifice of the few provides for the prosperity of many.

> The tragedy of the many reveals the greed of a few.

Practice

Write a sentence using antithesis about someone you respect, such as a family member or a friend.

Find an idea to emphasize.

_____

Generate contrasting ideas (words or phrases).

_____

Select a contrasting idea that emphasizes your original idea.

_____

Make the second idea parallel to the first, and rewrite your sentence using these two contrasting ideas in parallel form.

_____

Next, write a sentence using antithesis about something you can see outside.

Find an idea to emphasize.

_____

Generate contrasting ideas (words or phrases).

_____

Select a contrasting idea that emphasizes your original idea.

_____

Make the second idea parallel to the first, and rewrite your sentence using these two contrasting ideas in parallel form.

_____

_____

Write a sentence using antithesis about a character in a favorite book.

Find an idea to emphasize.

_____

Generate contrasting ideas (words or phrases).

_____

Select a contrasting idea that emphasizes your original idea.

_____

Make the second idea parallel to the first and rewrite your sentence using these two contrasting ideas in parallel form.

_____

_____

Now add your own examples of antithesis to Essay Five.

ESSAY SIX

Essay Six Invention

CIRCUMSTANCE

Write your Issue.

_____

Describe the situation (the time and location in which your Issue needs to be decided).

_____

Use the chart below to list actions and events that occur at the same time as, in different locations from, your Issue.

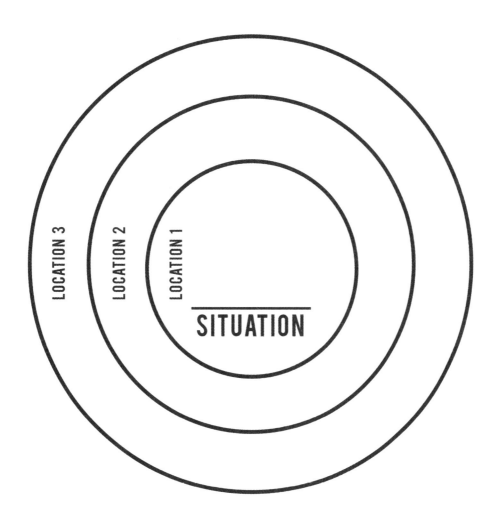

Essay Six Arrangement A
GUIDE TO REFUTATION

Write your Thesis statement.

_____

Write your Counter-Thesis.

_____

Choose one Proof that supports the Counter-Thesis.

_____

List three Sub-Proofs.

_____

_____

_____

Explain why this Proof is not persuasive.

_____

_____

_____

Choose a second Proof for the Counter-Thesis.

_____

Choose three Sub-Proofs.

_____

_____

_____

Explain why this Proof is not persuasive.

_____

_____

_____

Essay Six Arrangement B

BASIC PERSUASIVE ESSAY WITH REFUTATION

Write your Issue.

_____

Thesis & Proof

Review your Invention and decide whether you will support the Affirmative or Negative case. Rewrite the Issue as a Thesis statement.

_____

Write the first Proof for your Thesis.

_____

List three Sub-Proofs that support your first Proof.

_____

_____

_____

Write the second Proof for your Thesis.

_____

List three Sub-Proofs that support your second Proof.

_____

_____

_____

Write the third Proof for your Thesis

_____

List three Sub-Proofs that support your third Proof.

_____
_____
_____

Refutation

Write the Counter-Thesis. _____

Write the first Counter-Proof. _____

_____

List the three Sub-Proofs for the first Counter-Proof. _____

_____

_____

State why this Counter-proof is not persuasive. _____

_____

Write the second Counter-Proof. _____

_____

List the three Sub-Proofs for the second Counter-Proof. _____

_____

_____

State why this Counter-proof is not persuasive. _____

_____

Summarize your complete Refutation:

Counter-Proof 1: _____

Counter-Proof 2: _____

Refutation statement:

_____

Conclusion
Summarize your argument

Repeat your Thesis.

_____

Repeat the main Proofs. _____

_____

_____

_____

Amplification

It matters to _____

because _____

Division
Clarifying the Argument

State the agreement between you and your opponent.

_____

_____

State the two positions that can be taken.

Affirmative _____

Negative _____

Distribution

Write your Thesis.

_____

Add the Enumeration.

_____

List your three main Proofs.

_____

_____

_____

Introduction
Introduce your argument

Choose and add the Exordium.

_____

_____

_____

_____

Essay Six Arrangement Template

BASIC PERSUASIVE ESSAY

Transcribe your outline onto a separate page, imitating the template provided below. Do not use complete sentences. Replace lines that have an asterisk with *your* information from the Arrangement Worksheet on the previous pages.

I. Introduction

    A. Exordium*

    B. Division

        1. Agreement*

        2. Disagreement

            a. Thesis*

            b. Counter-Thesis*

    C. Distribution

        1. Thesis*

        2. Enumeration*

        3. Exposition*

            a. Proof I*

            b. Proof II*

            c. Proof III*

II. Proof

    A. Proof I*

        1. Sub-Proof 1*

        2. Sub-Proof 2*

        3. Sub-Proof 3*

    B. Proof II*

        1. Sub-Proof 1*

        2. Sub-Proof 2*

        3. Sub-Proof 3*

    C. Proof III*

        1. Sub-Proof 1*

        2. Sub-Proof 2*

        3. Sub-Proof 3*

III. Refutation

    A. Counter-Thesis*

    B. Counter-Proof 1*

        1. Summary of support for reason 1*

        2. Inadequacy of reason 1*

    C. Counter-Proof 2*

        1. Summary of support for reason 2 *

        2. Inadequacy of reason 2*

    D. Summary of Refutation*

IV. Conclusion

    A. Thesis*

    B. Summary of Proof

        1. Proof I*

        2. Proof II*

        3. Proof III*

    C. Amplification

        1. To whom it matters

        2. Why it matters

Essay Six Elocution
SIMILE

Definition

Simile is a trope that makes an explicit comparison of two things different in kind but sharing a common characteristic. Similes use "like," "as," or "seems" to make a comparison explicit.

Examples

From Psalm 42:1

"As the hart panteth after the water brooks, so panteth my soul after thee, O God."

From Proverbs 11:22

"As a jewel of gold in a swine's snout, so is a fair woman which is without discretion."

From C.S. Lewis's *The Lion, the Witch, and the Wardrobe*

"Edmund saw the drop for a second in midair, shining like a diamond."

73

> **From Homer's *The Iliad***
>
> "Like a man in his helplessness who, crossing a great plain, stands at the edge of a fast-running river that dashes seaward, and watches it thundering into white water, and leaps a pace backward, so now Tydeus' son gave back."

> **From Homer's *The Iliad***
>
> "Like some ox of the herd pre-eminent among the others, a bull, who stands conspicuous in the huddling cattle; such was the son of Atreus as Zeus made him that day."

Steps to Creating Similes

1. Write the term that you'd like to describe with a simile. *Example: bird*

2. Select a characteristic or quality of this term.
   Examples: loud, beautiful, feathered, singer, loud-squawker

3. Choose a different kind of thing that shares this characteristic and join it to your first term with a comparative word such as "like" or "as".

   Examples: The bird is like a train / The bird is as loud as a train / Like a train rumbling down the tracks, the bird's squawking goes on and on.

Student Examples

> The bird is like a train. OR The bird is as loud as a train.

> My cat is like a pillow. OR My cat is as fluffy as a pillow.

The mountains are like medicine for my soul.

As the Emperor lay ill, Death sat as a heavy weight on his chest, tormenting him with mocking visions of the Emperor's wrongs in life and taking away his treasures: his sword, his banner, his crown, and now his life.

Practice

1. Choose something you can see and hold and describe it using simile.

    Term: _____

    Quality: _____

    Thing of a different kind that shares one quality:

    _____

    Simile:

    _____

2. Write a simile about a character in a book.

    Term: _____

    Quality: _____

    Thing of a different kind that shares one quality:

    _____

    Simile:

    _____

3. Practice writing several similes for terms from your essay.

Term: _____

Quality: _____

Thing of a different kind that shares one quality:

_____

Simile:

_____

Now add your own examples of simile to Essay Six.

ESSAY SEVEN

Essay Seven Invention
RELATION: CAUSE & EFFECT

Write your Issue.

_____

1. Describe the situation in which the actor finds himself.

_____

2. List several actions or events that preceded this situation.

_____

_____

_____

_____

_____

3. Select and circle several causes or probable causes of the situation.

4. List several actions or events that followed or will likely follow the Affirmative decision.

_____

_____

_____

_____

5. List several actions or events that followed or will likely follow the Negative decision.

_____

_____

_____

_____

_____

6. Select and circle several effects or probable effects of each decision.

**Review your I column, and move
any appropriate items to the A or N.**

Essay Seven Arrangement A
A GUIDE TO NARRATIO

Write your Thesis.

_____

Describe the situation in which the actor finds himself:

- *Time*

  _____

- *Place*

  _____

- *Actors*

  _____

What action or decision led to this situation?

_____

What caused the action or decision above? List a sequence of actions, events, and/or decisions that caused the situation.

_____

_____

_____

_____

_____

_____

Select the causes to include in your Narratio.

_____

_____

_____

Essay Seven Arrangement B
BASIC PERSUASIVE ESSAY WITH NARRATIO

Write your issue.

_____

Thesis & Proof

Review your invention, and decide whether you will support the Affirmative or Negative case. Rewrite the Issue as a Thesis statement.

_____

Write the first Proof for your Thesis.

_____

List three Sub-Proofs that support your first Proof.

_____

_____

_____

Write the second Proof for your Thesis.

_____

List three Sub-Proofs that support your second Proof.

_____

_____

_____

Write the third Proof for your Thesis.

List three Sub-Proofs that support your third Proof.

_____

_____

_____

Refutation

Write the Counter-Thesis. _____

Write the first Counter-Proof. _____

_____

List the three Sub-Proofs for the first Counter-Proof. _____

_____

_____

State why this is not persuasive. _____

_____

Write the second Counter-Proof. _____

_____

List the three Sub-proofs for the second Counter-Proof. _____

_____

_____

State why this is not persuasive. _____

_____

Summarize your complete Refutation.

Counter-Proof 1: _____

Counter-Proof 2: _____

Refutation Statement: _____

Conclusion
Summarize your argument

Repeat your Thesis.

_____

Repeat the main Proofs.

_____

_____

_____

Amplification

It matters to_____

because _____

Division
Clarifying the Argument

State the agreement between you and your opponent.

_____

_____

State the two position that can be taken.

Affirmative _____

Negative _____

Distribution

Write your Thesis.

_____

Add the Enumeration.

_____

List your three main Proofs.

_____

_____

_____

Narratio
Statement of Facts

Outline the situation: time, place, and people.

_____

_____

_____

List the causes of the situation.

_____

_____

_____

Introduction
Introduce your argument

Choose and add an Exordium.

_____

_____

_____

_____

Essay Seven Arrangement Template

COMPLETE PERSUASIVE ESSAY

Transcribe your outline onto a separate page, using the template provided below. Replace lines that have an asterisk with *your* information from the Arrangement Worksheet on the previous pages.

I. Introduction
    A. Exordium*
    B. Narratio*
        1. Situation*
        2. Actions*
    C. Division
        1. Agreement*
        2. Disagreement
            a. Thesis*
            b. Counter-Thesis*
    D. Distribution
        1. Thesis*
        2. Enumeration*
        3. Exposition*
            a. Proof I*
            b. Proof II*
            c. Proof III*

II. Proof
    A. Proof I*
        1. Sub-proof 1*
        2. Sub-proof 2*
        3. Sub-proof 3*
    B. Proof II*
        1. Sub-proof 1*
        2. Sub-proof 2*
        3. Sub-proof 3*
    C. Proof III*
        1. Sub-proof 1*
        2. Sub-proof 2*
        3. Sub-proof 3*

III. Refutation
    A. Counter-Thesis*
    B. Counter-Proof 1*
        1. Summary of support for reason 1 *
        2. Inadequacy of reason 1*
    C. Counter-Proof 2*
        1. Summary of support for reason 2 *
        2. Inadequacy of reason 2*
    D. **Summary of Refutation***

IV. Conclusion
    A. Thesis*
    B. Summary of Proof
        1. Proof I*
        2. Proof II*
        3. Proof III*
    C. Amplification
        1. To whom it matters*
        2. Why it matters to that person or group*
        3. Why it matters to that person or group*

Essay Seven Elocution
ALLITERATION

Definition

*Alliteration is a scheme that uses the repetition of adjacent or closely connected **consonant** sounds.*

Examples

From Peter Piper

"**P**eter **P**iper **p**icked a **p**eck of **p**ickled **p**eppers;
A **p**eck of **p**ickled **p**eppers **P**eter **P**iper **p**icked.
If **P**eter **P**iper **p**icked a **p**eck of **p**ickled **p**eppers,
Where's the **p**eck of **p**ickled **p**eppers **P**eter **P**iper **p**icked?"

From Henry Wadsworth Longfellow's *Paul Revere's Ride*

"Where the river widens to meet the **b**ay,--
A line of **b**lack that **b**ends and floats
On the rising tide like a **b**ridge of **b**oats."

From Samuel Taylor Coleridge's *The Rime of the Ancient Mariner*

"For the sky and the sea,
and the sea and the sky . . ."

From John F. Kennedy's Inaugural Address

"With a good conscience our only sure reward, with history the final judge of our deeds, let us go forth to lead the land we love, asking His blessing and His help, but knowing that here on earth God's work must truly be our own."

From *Beowulf*

"Hot hearted Beowulf was bent upon battle."

From Alfred Lord Tennyson's *Sir Galahad*

"Fly o'er waste fens and windy fields."

From Robert Frost's "The Death of a Hired Man"

"Mary sat musing on the lamp-flame at the table
Waiting for Warren. When she heard his
step..."

Steps to Writing Alliteration

1. Select a seed-word to use in your alliteration.
2. Identify the consonant sound to repeat.
3. Generate more words that begin with the same consonant sound and fit your sentence.
4. Rewrite the sentence using words from your list.

Student Examples

Standing silently, Aeneas sailed sadly away from Troy.

Longing for a mission, Edmund mindlessly followed the mean tyrant of Narnia.

Edmund caused careless calamity for his siblings and for all of Narnia.

Practice

1. Use alliteration in a sentence about someone you know, such a family member or friend.

   _____

   _____

2. Use alliteration in a sentence about something you can see outside.

   _____

   _____

3. Use alliteration in a sentence about a character in a favorite book.

_____

_____

**Now add your own examples of
alliteration to Essay Seven.**

ESSAY EIGHT

Essay Eight Invention
TESTIMONY

There are two kinds of testimony you will consider in this exercise: the eyewitness and the character witness.

- ❖ An **eye witness** is someone who observed the action or situation with which the Issue is concerned.

- ❖ A **character witness** has observed a person who is involved in the situation. The character witness has observed this person in a different situation and bears witness to his character.

The witness will bear witness to the actor and actions; the witness is not a judge.

Describe the situation of the Issue.

_____

Witness #1: Eyewitness

1. Name an eyewitness.

_____

2. What has this witness seen the actor do or experience in this situation?

_____

_____

3. How reliable do you consider this witness? Check one.

❏ Mostly Reliable

❏ Mostly Unreliable

4. Name an additional eyewitness.

_____

_____

5. What has this witness seen?

_____

_____

6. How reliable do you consider this witness? Check one.

❏ Mostly Reliable

❏ Mostly Unreliable

7. Repeat with any additional eyewitnesses.

Witness #2: Character Witness

1. Write the name of a person who knows something about the character of an actor(s) in this situation.

_____

2. About whose character can he testify?

_____

_____

3. What did the witness observe and in what circumstances did he observe it?

_____

_____

4. What does that suggest about the character of the actor?

_____

_____

5. How do these observations relate to the situation?

_____

_____

6. How reliable do you consider the witness? Check one.

    ❑ Mostly unreliable
    ❑ Mostly reliable

**Review your I column, and move any
appropriate items to the A or N columns.**

Essay Eight Elocution
METAPHOR

Definition

Metaphor, a trope, is an indirect comparison of two different kinds of things (indirect- i.e., you do not use "like" or "as").

Examples

From Shakespeare's *A Comedy of Errors*

"A man may break a word with you, sir, and words are but wind."

From John 15:5

"I am the vine, ye are the branches . . ."

From Psalm 23:1

"The Lord is my shepherd . . ."

From John Donne

"Reason is our soul's left hand, faith her right."

From Psalm 5:9

"Their throat is an open sepulcher; with their tongues they have used deceit."

From William Shakespeare's Sonnet 147

"My reason, the physician to my love,
Angry that his prescriptions are not kept,
Hath left me. ."

Steps to Creating a Metaphor

a) Select a thing that you will develop with a metaphor.
b) Identify a trait or action of the thing selected.
c) Identify a thing of a different kind that possesses or seems to possess the same trait or is marked by the same action(the more concrete and different from the first thing, the better).
d) Combine the two things, stating that one thing is the other.

Student Examples

My books are my airplanes.

That phone is a flock of birds.

Practice

Write a metaphor about someone you know, such as a family member or a friend.

Identify someone to write a metaphor about.

_____

Identify a trait or action displayed by that person.

_____

_____

Identify a thing of a different kind that shares that trait or action.

_____

Completed Metaphor:

_____

_____

_____

Write a metaphor about something you can see or imagine.

Identify something to write a metaphor about.

_____

Identify a trait or action displayed by that thing.

_____

_____

Identify a thing of a different kind that shares that trait or action.

_____

Completed Metaphor:

_____

_____

_____

Write a metaphor about a character in a favorite book.

Identify a character to write a metaphor about.

_____

Identify a trait or action displayed by that character.

_____

_____

Identify a different character that shares that trait or action.

_____

Completed Metaphor:

_____

_____

_____

**Now add your own examples of
metaphor to Essay Eight.**

ESSAY NINE

Essay Nine Elocution
ASSONANCE

Definition

Assonance is a scheme in which one vowel sound is
repeated in adjacent or closely connected words.

Examples

> ### From Shelley's Sonnet "England in 1819"
>
> "An old mad, blind, despised, and dying king—
> Princes, the dregs of their dull race, who flow
> Through public scorn—mud from a muddy spring."

> ### From W.B. Yeats' "Byzantium"
>
> "Those images that yet,
> Fresh images beget,
> That dolphin-torn, that gong-tormented sea"

> **From Robert Frost's "After Apple-Picking"**
>
> "Stem end and blossom end,
> And every fleck of russet showing clear . . ."

> **From J. R. R. Tolkien's *The Two Towers***
>
> "I make the earth shake as I tramp through the grass;
> trees crack as I pass."

Steps to Creating Assonance

1. Select a seed-word whose vowel sound you wish to repeat.
2. Identify the vowel sound.
3. Generate more words that include the same vowel sound.
4. Rewrite the sentence using words from your list. Make any necessary changes to be sure your sentence makes sense.

Student Examples

> Achilles yawned and thought--he was their rock and their rod, on top of their applause.

> If Anne dreams, she sees the peace she seeks and needs.

> In time, if he rides, keeps good line, feels bright, hits the side—he can find a sign and do right.

Practice

1. Write a sentence using assonance about someone you know, such as a family member or a friend.

THE LOST TOOLS OF WRITING LEVEL ONE

_____

_____

2. Write a sentence using assonance about something you can see outside.

_____

_____

_____

3. Write a sentence using assonance about a character in a favorite book.

_____

_____

_____

**Now add your own examples
of assonance to Essay Nine.**

SELF-EDIT CHECKLISTS

ESSAY ONE CHECKLIST
RUDIMENTARY PERSUASIVE ESSAY: OUTLINE TO TEXT

- ☐ Essay follows Template 1

- ☐ Introduction has a Thesis with Enumeration and Exposition

- ☐ The first Proof begins as "The first reason..." followed by the Thesis and Proof

- ☐ The second Proof begins as "The second reason..." followed by the Thesis and Proof

- ☐ The third Proof begins as "The third reason..." followed by the Thesis and Proof

- ☐ Conclusion restates the Thesis and summarizes the Proofs in a single sentence without the Enumeration

- ☐ Checked spelling of uncertain words in a dictionary

- ☐ Checked grammar
  - ○ Verb tense is consistent
  - ○ Subjects and verbs agree
  - ○ Repaired fragments and run-ons

- ☐ Checked punctuation
  - ○ Capital letters are used correctly
  - ○ Commas, colons, semi-colons, and hyphens are used correctly
  - ○ Correct end punctuation is used

ESSAY TWO CHECKLIST
INTRODUCTORY PERSUASIVE ESSAY

- ☐ Essay follows Template 2

- ☐ Introduction has a Thesis with Enumeration and Exposition

- ☐ Main Proofs are written clearly

- ☐ Each main Proof is supported by three Sub-proofs

- ☐ Conclusion restates the Thesis and summarizes the Proofs in a single sentence without the Enumeration

- ☐ Marked and labeled scheme 1—Parallelism: words

- ☐ Checked spelling of uncertain words in a dictionary

- ☐ Checked grammar
    - o Verb tense is consistent
    - o Subjects and verbs agree
    - o Repaired fragments and run-ons

- ☐ Checked punctuation
    - o Capital letters are used correctly
    - o Commas, colons, semicolons, and hyphens are used correctly
    - o Correct end punctuation is used

ESSAY THREE CHECKLIST
BASIC PERSUASIVE ESSAY: EXORDIUM

- ❏ Essay follows Template 3

- ❏ Exordium is added to the beginning of the essay

- ❏ Introduction has a Thesis with Enumeration and Exposition

- ❏ Main Proofs are written clearly and supported with Sub-proofs

- ❏ Repaired weak verbs
  - o Vague
  - o Passive

- ❏ Marked and labeled scheme 1—Parallelism: words

- ❏ Checked spelling of uncertain words in a dictionary

- ❏ Checked grammar
  - o Verb tense is consistent
  - o Subjects and verbs agree
  - o Repaired fragments and run-ons

- ❏ Checked punctuation
  - o Capital letters are used correctly
  - o Commas, colons, semicolons, and hyphens are used correctly
  - o Correct end punctuation is used

ESSAY FOUR CHECKLIST
BASIC PERSUASIVE ESSAY: AMPLIFICATION

- ☐ Essay follows Template 4

- ☐ Amplification is added to the end of the essay

- ☐ Main Proofs are written clearly and supported with Sub-proofs

- ☐ Proofs are parallel

- ☐ Exordium is added to the beginning of the essay

- ☐ Introduction has a Thesis with Enumeration and Exposition.

- ☐ Repaired weak verbs
  - ○ Vague
  - ○ Passive

- ☐ Marked and labeled each scheme
  - ○ Parallelism 1: words
  - ○ Parallelism 2: phrases or clauses

- ☐ Checked spelling of uncertain words in a dictionary

- ☐ Checked grammar
  - ○ Verb tense is consistent
  - ○ Subjects and verbs agree
  - ○ Repaired fragments and run-ons

- ☐ Checked punctuation
  - ○ Capital letters are used correctly
  - ○ Commas, colons, semicolons, and hyphens are used correctly
  - ○ Correct end punctuation is used
  - ○ Quotation marks are used correctly

ESSAY FIVE CHECKLIST
BASIC PERSUASIVE ESSAY : DIVISION AND DISTRIBUTION

- ☐ Essay follows Template 5

- ☐ Division is added to the essay

- ☐ Main Proofs are written clearly and supported with Sub-proofs

- ☐ Proofs are parallel

- ☐ Amplification is added to the end of the essay

- ☐ Introduction has a Thesis with Enumeration and Exposition

- ☐ Exordium is added to the beginning of the essay

- ☐ Repaired weak verbs
  - o Vague
  - o Passive

- ☐ Marked and labeled each scheme
  - o Parallelism 1 and 2
  - o Antithesis

- ☐ Checked spelling of uncertain words in a dictionary

- ☐ Checked grammar
  - o Verb tense is consistent
  - o Subjects and verbs agree
  - o Repaired fragments and run-ons

- ☐ Checked punctuation
  - o Capital letters are used correctly
  - o Commas, colons, semicolons, and hyphens are used correctly
  - o Correct end punctuation is used
  - o Quotation marks are used correctly

ESSAY SIX CHECKLIST
BASIC PERSUASIVE ESSAY:REFUTATION

- ☐ Essay follows Template 6

- ☐ Refutation is added to the essay

- ☐ Main Proofs are written clearly and supported with Sub-proofs

- ☐ Proofs are parallel

- ☐ Amplification is added to the end of the essay

- ☐ Introduction has a Thesis with Enumeration and Exposition

- ☐ Division is added to the essay

- ☐ Exordium is added to the beginning of the essay

- ☐ Repaired weak verbs
  - o Vague
  - o Passive
- ☐ Marked and labeled each scheme
  - o Parallelism 1 and 2
  - o Antithesis
- ☐ Marked and labeled each trope
  - o Simile
- ☐ Checked spelling of uncertain words in a dictionary

- ☐ Checked grammar
  - o Verb tense is consistent
  - o Subjects and verbs agree
  - o Repaired fragments and run-ons
- ☐ Checked punctuation
  - o Capital letters are used correctly
  - o Commas, colons, semicolons, and hyphens are used correctly
  - o Correct end punctuation is used
  - o Quotation marks are used correctly

ESSAY SEVEN CHECKLIST
COMPLETE PERSUASIVE ESSAY: NARRATIO

- ❑ Essay follows Template 7

- ❑ Narratio is added to the essay

- ❑ Refutation is added to the essay

- ❑ Main Proofs are written clearly and supported with Sub-proofs

- ❑ Proofs are parallel

- ❑ Amplification is added to the end of the essay

- ❑ Introduction has a Thesis with Enumeration and Exposition

- ❑ Division is added to the essay

- ❑ Exordium is added to the beginning of the essay

- ❑ Repaired weak verbs
  - ○ Vague
  - ○ Passive
- ❑ Marked and labeled each scheme
  - ○ Parallelism 1 and 2
  - ○ Antithesis
  - ○ Alliteration
- ❑ Marked and labeled each trope
  - ○ Simile
- ❑ Checked spelling of uncertain words in a dictionary

- ❑ Checked grammar
  - ○ Verb tense is consistent
  - ○ Subjects and verbs agree
  - ○ Repaired fragments and run-ons
- ❑ Checked punctuation
  - ○ Capital letters are used correctly
  - ○ Commas, colons, semicolons, and hyphens are used correctly
  - ○ Correct end punctuation is used
  - ○ Quotation marks are used correctly

ESSAY EIGHT CHECKLIST
COMPLETE PERSUASIVE ESSAY: REVIEW AND PRACTICE

- ❏ Essay follows Template 8

- ❏ Narratio is added to the essay

- ❏ Refutation is added to the essay

- ❏ Main Proofs are written clearly and supported with Sub-proofs

- ❏ Proofs are parallel

- ❏ Amplification is added to the end of the essay

- ❏ Introduction has a Thesis with Enumeration and Exposition.

- ❏ Division is added to the essay

- ❏ Exordium is added to the beginning of the essay

- ❏ Repaired weak verbs
  - o Vague
  - o Passive
- ❏ Marked and labeled each scheme
  - o Parallelism
  - o Antithesis
  - o Alliteration
- ❏ Marked and labeled each trope
  - o Simile
  - o Metaphor

- ❏ Checked spelling of uncertain words in a dictionary

- ❏ Checked grammar
  - o Verb tense is consistent
  - o Subjects and verbs agree
  - o Repaired fragments and run-ons

- ❏ Checked punctuation
  - o Capital letters are used correctly
  - o Commas, colons, semicolons, and hyphens are used correctly
  - o Correct end punctuation is used
  - o Quotation marks are used correctly

ESSAY NINE CHECKLIST
COMPLETE PERSUASIVE ESSAY: REVIEW AND PRACTICE

- ❏ Essay follows Template 9

- ❏ Narratio is added to the essay

- ❏ Refutation is added to the essay

- ❏ Main Proofs are written clearly and supported with Sub-proofs

- ❏ Proofs are parallel

- ❏ Amplification is added to the end of the essay

- ❏ Introduction has a thesis with Enumeration and Exposition

- ❏ Division is added to the essay

- ❏ Exordium is added to the beginning of the essay

- ❏ Repaired weak verbs
  - ○ Vague
  - ○ Passive
- ❏ Marked and labeled each scheme
  - ○ Parallelism
  - ○ Antithesis
  - ○ Alliteration
  - ○ Assonance
- ❏ Marked and labeled each trope
  - ○ Simile
  - ○ Metaphor
- ❏ Checked spelling of uncertain words in a dictionary

- ❏ Checked grammar
  - ○ Verb tense is consistent
  - ○ Subjects and verbs agree
  - ○ Repaired fragments and run-ons
- ❏ Checked punctuation
  - ○ Capital letters are used correctly
  - ○ Commas, colons, semicolons, and hyphens are used correctly
  - ○ Correct end punctuation is used.
  - ○ Quotation marks are used correctly

SAMPLE ESSAYS

ESSAY ONE

SAMPLE ESSAY A

Edmund should not have followed the White Witch for three reasons: Edmund's sister Lucy warned him that the White Witch was evil, he should have seen that the White Witch was evil, and he acted in secret.

The first reason Edmund should not have followed the White Witch is that his sister Lucy warned him that the White Witch was evil. The second reason Edmund should not have followed the White Witch is that he should have seen that the White Witch was evil. The third reason Edmund should not have followed the White Witch is that he acted in secret.

Edmund should not have followed the White Witch because his sister Lucy warned him that the White Witch was evil, he should have seen that the White Witch was evil, and he acted in secret.

SAMPLE ESSAY A

Della should cut her hair for three reasons: she had something she could sacrifice, for love, and it was Christmas.

The first reason Della should cut her hair is she had something she could sacrifice. The second reason Della should cut her hair is for love. The third reason Della should cut her hair is it was Christmas.

Della should cut her hair because she had something she could sacrifice, for love, and it was Christmas.

ESSAY TWO

SAMPLE ESSAY A

Edmund should not have followed the White Witch for three reasons: Edmund *purposely ignored a warning, carelessly overlooked the White Witch,* and *secretly followed Lucy* into Narnia.

The first reason Edmund should not have followed the White Witch is that he purposely ignored a warning. **The White Witch introduced herself to Edmund as "The Queen of Narnia," but Lucy, who had already met with real creatures in Narnia, called her the "White Witch." We know from fairy tales and literature that witches are evil. Therefore, he should not have followed evil.**

The second reason that Edmund should not have followed the White Witch is that he carelessly overlooked the White Witch. **Initially, the White Witch was very cruel to Edmund, and his first instinct was to be scared of her. She fed him Turkish Delight only when she wanted to get something from him. Edmund, with his own eyes, should have seen from this interaction that the White Witch was evil.**

The third reason Edmund should not have followed the White Witch is that he secretly followed Lucy into Narnia. **In his very core, Edmund knew that he was doing wrong because he secretly left his siblings and the Beavers and did not discuss his plan with them. Instead of acting openly, he snuck away, probably because they would have not gone along with his plan. Edmund knew that he was betraying his family and innocent creatures.**

Edmund should not have followed the White Witch because he purposely ignored a warning, carelessly overlooked the White Witch, and secretly followed Lucy into Narnia.

SAMPLE ESSAY B

Della should cut her hair for three reasons: to sacrifice, to show love, and to celebrate Christmas.

The first reason Della should cut her hair is to sacrifice. **Her long hair is the most valuable possession she owns**. Della derives great pleasure from catching a glimpse of herself in the small mirror in her flat. **To cut her hair will be a permanent decision**. Her hair will most likely not grow back to that great length. **She may not have much money, but she has a marketable commodity**. By giving up her most precious possession, she will change her looks dramatically.

The second reason Della should cut her hair is to show love. **In the throes of young love, this precious wife desires to show her husband the depth of her love for him. Throughout the story Jim is pictured as a caring provider, tenderly seeing to his wife. It makes perfect sense that Della would want to find a way to return that commitment with a gesture of her own.**

The third reason Della should cut her hair is to celebrate Christmas. **As the season of giving surrounds her, Della is likely reminded everywhere she goes of the approaching holiday. In a large city such as New York, advertisements, shop windows, and newspapers would all serve as reminders that while everyone else may be shopping for his special someone, Della can't. By cutting her hair she can give Jim not only a gift, but also a perfect complement to the family heirloom.**

Della should sell her hair to sacrifice, show love, and celebrate Christmas.

ESSAY THREE

SAMPLE ESSAY A

What would you do if a pale, white, icy lady asked you to follow her? In *The Lion, The Witch and The Wardrobe*, Edmund had to make this very decision. Edmund should not have followed the White Witch for three reasons: Edmund purposely ignored a warning, carelessly overlooked the White Witch, and secretly followed Lucy into Narnia.

The first reason Edmund should not have followed the White Witch is that he purposely ignored a warning. The White Witch introduced herself to Edmund as "The Queen of Narnia," but Lucy, who had already met with real creatures in Narnia, called her the "White Witch." We know from fairy tales and literature that witches are evil. Therefore he should not have followed evil.

The second reason that Edmund should not have followed the White Witch is that he carelessly overlooked the White Witch. Initially, the White Witch was very cruel to Edmund, and his first instinct was to be scared of her. She fed him Turkish Delight only when she wanted to get something from him. Edmund, with his own eyes, should have seen from this interaction that the White Witch was evil.

The third reason Edmund should not have followed the White Witch is that he secretly followed Lucy into Narnia. From his very core, Edmund knew that he was doing wrong because he secretly left his siblings and the Beavers and did not discuss his plan with them. Instead of acting openly, he snuck away, probably because they would have not gone along with his plan. Edmund knew that he was betraying his family and innocent creatures.

Edmund should not have followed the White Witch because he purposely ignored a warning, carelessly overlooked the White Witch, and secretly followed Lucy into Narnia.

SAMPLE ESSAY B

Imagine giving up your most precious possession. In the short story "The Gift of the Magi" by O. Henry, the main character was faced with this very challenge. Della should cut her hair for three reasons: to sacrifice, to show love, and to celebrate Christmas.

The first reason Della should cut her hair is *to sacrifice*. Her long hair is the most valuable possession she owns. Della derives great pleasure from catching a glimpse of herself in the small mirror in her flat. To cut her hair off will be a permanent decision. Her hair, most likely, will not grow back to that great length. She may not have much money, but she has a marketable commodity. By giving up her most precious possession, she will change her looks dramatically.

The second reason Della should cut her hair is to show love. In the throes of young love, this precious wife desires to show her husband the depth of her love for him. Throughout the story, the author pictures Jim as a caring provider, tenderly seeing to his wife. It makes perfect sense that Della would want to find a way to return that commitment with a gesture of her own.

The third reason Della should cut her hair is to celebrate Christmas. As the season of giving surrounds her, festive decorations and fancy shop windows remind Della of the approaching holiday. In a large city such as New York, advertisements, shop windows, and newspapers would all serve as reminders that while everyone else may be shopping for his special someone, Della has no means to do so. By cutting her hair she not only can give Jim a gift, but also a perfect complement to the family heirloom.

Della should sell her hair to sacrifice, show love, and celebrate Christmas.

ESSAY FOUR

SAMPLE ESSAY A

What would you do if a pale, white, icy lady asked you to follow her? *In The Lion, The Witch, and The Wardrobe,* Edmund had to make this very decision. Edmund should not have followed the White Witch for three reasons: Edmund **purposely ignored a warning, carelessly overlooked the White Witch, and secretly followed Lucy into Narnia**.

The first reason Edmund should not have followed the White Witch is that he purposely ignored a warning. The White Witch introduced herself to Edmund as "The Queen of Narnia," but Lucy, who had already met with real creatures in Narnia, called her the "White Witch." We know from fairy tales and literature that witches are evil. Therefore he should not have followed evil.

The second reason that Edmund should not have followed the White Witch is that he carelessly overlooked the White Witch. Initially, the White Witch was very cruel to Edmund, and his first instinct was to be scared of her. She fed him Turkish Delight only when she wanted to get something from him. Edmund, with his own eyes, should have seen from this interaction that the White Witch was evil.

The third reason Edmund should not have followed the White Witch was that he secretly followed Lucy into Narnia. From his very core, Edmund knew that he was doing wrong because he secretly left his siblings and the Beavers and did not discuss his plan with them. Instead of acting openly, he snuck away, probably because they would have not gone along with his plan. Edmund knew that he was betraying his family and innocent creatures.

Edmund should not have followed the White Witch because he purposely ignored a warning, carelessly overlooked the White Witch, and secretly followed Lucy into Narnia. **Edmund caused tremendous** trouble not only for himself, but—even worse—for his siblings and for all of Narnia.

SAMPLE ESSAY B

Imagine giving up your most precious possession. In the short story "The Gift of the Magi" by O. Henry, the main character was faced with this very decision. Della should cut her hair for three reasons: **to sacrifice, to show love, and to celebrate Christmas.**

The first reason Della should cut her hair is *to* sacrifice. Her long hair is the most valuable possession she owns. Della derives great pleasure from catching a glimpse of herself in the small mirror in her flat. To cut her hair off will be a permanent decision. Her hair, most likely, will not grow back to that great length. She may not have much money, but she has a marketable commodity. By giving up her most precious possession, she will change her looks dramatically.

The second reason Della should cut her hair is to show love. In the throes of young love, this precious wife desires to show her husband the depth of her love for him. Throughout the story, the author pictures Jim as a caring provider, tenderly seeing to his wife. It makes perfect sense that Della would want to find a way to return that commitment with a gesture of her own.

The third reason Della should cut her hair is to celebrate Christmas. As the season of giving surrounds her, festive decorations and fancy shop windows remind Della of the approaching holiday. In a large city such as New York, advertisements, shop windows, and newspapers would all serve as reminders that while everyone else may be shopping for his special someone, Della has no means to do so. By cutting her hair she not only can give Jim a gift, but also a perfect complement to the family heirloom.

Della should sell her hair to sacrifice, show love, and celebrate Christmas. **This matters to our friends and family, members of our community, as we all need a picture of what Christmas is all about. What matters is not the value of the gifts one receives, but of the gifts one gives**

ESSAY FIVE

SAMPLE ESSAY A

What would you do if a pale, white, icy lady asked you to follow her? In *The Lion, The Witch, and The Wardrobe,* Edmund had to make this very decision. **Everyone agrees that Edmund followed the White Witch, but some believe that Edmund should have followed her and some believe that he should not have followed her.**

Edmund should not have followed the White Witch for three reasons: Edmund purposely ignored a warning, carelessly overlooked the White Witch, and secretly followed Lucy into Narnia.

The first reason Edmund should not have followed the White Witch is that he purposely ignored a warning. The White Witch introduced herself to Edmund as "The Queen of Narnia," but Lucy, who had already met with real creatures in Narnia, called her the "White Witch." We know from fairy tales and literature that witches are evil. Therefore he should not have followed evil.

The second reason that Edmund should not have followed the White Witch is that he carelessly overlooked the White Witch. Initially, the White Witch was very cruel to Edmund, and his first instinct was to be scared of her. She fed him Turkish Delight only when she wanted to get something from him. Edmund, with his own eyes, should have seen from this interaction that the White Witch was evil.

The third reason Edmund should not have followed the White Witch was that he secretly followed Lucy into Narnia. From his very core, Edmund knew that he was doing wrong because he secretly left his siblings and the Beavers and did not discuss his plan with them. **He could have been honest and open, but he chose to be deceitful and secretive--**probably because they would have not gone along with his plan. Edmund knew that he was betraying his family and innocent creatures.

Edmund should not have followed the White Witch because he purposely ignored a warning, carelessly overlooked the White Witch, and secretly followed Lucy into Narnia. Edmund caused tremendous trouble not only for himself, but—even worse—for his siblings and for all of Narnia.

SAMPLE ESSAY B

Imagine giving up your most precious possession. In the short story, "The Gift of the Magi" by O. Henry, the main character was faced with this very decision. **Everyone agrees that Della greatly desires to give a gift to her husband, Jim, for Christmas; however some feel Della should cut and sell her hair to pay for the gift, while others feel Della should not cut and sell her hair.**

Della should cut her hair for three reasons: to sacrifice, to show love, and to celebrate Christmas.

The first reason Della should cut her hair is to sacrifice. Her long hair is the most valuable possession she owns. Della derives great pleasure from catching a glimpse of herself in the small mirror in her flat.. To cut her hair off will be a permanent decision. Her hair, most likely, will not grow back to that great length. She may not have much money, but she has a marketable commodity. By giving up her most precious possession, she will change her looks dramatically.

The second reason Della should cut her hair is to show love. In the throes of young love, this precious wife desires to show her husband the depth of her love for him. Throughout the story, the author pictures Jim as a caring provider, tenderly seeing to his wife. It makes perfect sense that Della would want to find a way to return that commitment with a gesture of her own.

The third reason Della should cut her hair is to celebrate Christmas. As the season of giving surrounds her, festive decorations and fancy shop windows remind Della of the approaching holiday. In a large city such as New York, advertisements, shop windows, and newspapers would all serve as reminders that while everyone else may be shopping for his special someone, Della has no means to do so. By cutting her hair she not only can give Jim a gift, but also a perfect complement to the family heirloom.

Della should sell her hair to sacrifice, show love, and celebrate Christmas. This matters to our friends and family, members of our community as we all need a picture of what Christmas is all about. What matters is not the value of the gifts one receives, but of the gifts one gives.

ESSAY SIX

SAMPLE ESSAY A

What would you do if a pale, white, icy lady asked you to follow her? In *The Lion, The Witch, and The Wardrobe,* Edmund had to make this very decision. Everyone agrees that Edmund followed the White Witch, but some believe that Edmund should have followed her and some believe that Edmund should not have followed her.

Edmund should not have followed the White Witch for three reasons: Edmund purposely ignored a warning, carelessly overlooked the White Witch, and secretly followed Lucy into Narnia.

The first reason Edmund should not have followed the White Witch is that he purposely ignored a warning. The White Witch introduced herself to Edmund as "The Queen of Narnia," but Lucy, who had already met with real creatures in Narnia, called her the "White Witch." We know from fairy tales and literature that witches are evil. Therefore he should not have followed evil.

The second reason Edmund should not have followed the White Witch is that he carelessly overlooked the White Witch. Initially, the White Witch was very cruel to Edmund, and his first instinct was to be scared of her. She fed him Turkish Delight only when she wanted to get something from him, **like a fisherman feeds a worm on a hook to the fish he wants to catch and eat**. Edmund, with his own eyes, should have seen from this interaction that the White Witch was evil.

The third reason Edmund should not have followed the White Witch is that he secretly followed Lucy into Narnia. From his very core, Edmund knew that he was doing wrong because he secretly left his siblings and the Beavers and did not discuss his plan with them. He could have been honest and open, but he chose to be deceitful and secretive—probably because they would have not gone along with his plan. Edmund knew that he was betraying his family and innocent creatures.

Some people say that Edmund should have followed the White Witch. They argue that the White Witch took care of Edmund, feeding him Turkish Delight and speaking kindly to him. However, this idea is inadequate because we see the White Witch's true personality later. We see that she did not really care about Edmund, but that she simply wanted to take over Narnia. Feeding Edmund Turkish Delight and speaking kindly to him was just a means to reaching her evil goal.

In addition, people argue that Edmund should have followed the White Witch because he was alone and scared; thus he could not use proper judgment. This argument is also invalid because Edmund was not really alone. He had his trustworthy sister, Lucy, with

him, and she had already testified that the White Witch was evil. We know that Edmund followed the White Witch out of pride and selfish ambition.

Neither of these arguments—that the White Witch took care of Edmund, and that Edmund was alone and scared—would give Edmund any sufficient reason to follow the White Witch.

Edmund should not have followed the White Witch because he purposely ignored a warning, carelessly overlooked the White Witch, and secretly followed Lucy into Narnia. Edmund caused tremendous trouble, not only for himself, but—even worse—for his siblings and for all of Narnia.

SAMPLE ESSAY B

Imagine giving up your most precious possession. In the short story "The Gift of the Magi" by O. Henry, the main character was faced with this very decision. Everyone agrees that Della greatly desires to give a gift to her husband, Jim, for Christmas, however some feel Della should cut and sell her hair to pay for the gift while others feel Della should not cut and sell her hair.

Della should cut her hair for three reasons: to sacrifice, to show love, and to celebrate Christmas.

The first reason Della should cut her hair is to sacrifice. Her long hair is the most valuable possession she owns. Della derives great pleasure from catching a glimpse of herself in the small mirror in her flat. *She feels like a parading peacock*. To cut her hair off will be a permanent decision. Her hair, most likely, will not grow back to that great length. She may not have much money, but she has a marketable commodity. By giving up her most precious possession, she will change her looks dramatically.

The second reason Della should cut her hair is to show love. In the throes of young love, this precious wife desires to show her husband the depth of her love for him. Throughout the story, the author pictures Jim as a caring provider, tenderly seeing to his wife. It makes perfect sense that Della would want to find a way to return that commitment with a gesture of her own.

The third reason Della should cut her hair is to celebrate Christmas. As the season of giving surrounds her, festive decorations and fancy shop windows remind Della of the approaching holiday. In a large city such as New York, advertisements, shop windows, and newspapers would all serve as reminders that while everyone else may be shopping for his special someone, Della has no means to do so. By cutting her hair she not only can give Jim a gift, but also a perfect complement to the family heirloom.

Some claim that Della should not sell her hair. After all, what might her husband's reaction be? Jim might not like her new hairstyle, might not approve of her sacrifice, and might hurt his career by having a wife who looks like a "Coney Island chorus girl." But there is no evidence to support this assertion. Della claims that a new watch chain might in fact help his standing in the community. A husband who would willingly sacrifice his own precious possession surely would not chastise his wife for selling hers.

In addition, some argue that the couple's budget is reason enough to put any spare change into savings. How can they justify such an impractical gift in the face of their present poverty? Jim wears a shabby coat, his salary has recently been reduced, and Della must bargain with the grocers for any savings she can. This reasoning is faulty. Even in the midst of less than ideal circumstances, a grand generous gesture can serve to remind us of the value of true love and sacrifice. Appropriate to the season of giving, Della can give.

Thus, neither Jim's reaction nor the couple's budget is enough to dissuade Della from selling her beautiful, valuable hair.

Della should sell her hair to sacrifice, show love, and celebrate Christmas. This matters to our friends, family, and members of our community as we all need a picture of what Christmas.

ESSAY SEVEN

SAMPLE ESSAY A

What would you do if a pale, white, icy lady asked you to follow her? In *The Lion, The Witch, and The Wardrobe*, Edmund had to make this very decision

One day, while playing hide and seek with his brother and sisters, Edmund followed his younger sister, Lucy, through an old, forgotten wardrobe. Passing through the coats, he found himself in a different world, the world of Narnia. Immediately, Edmund was startled by an icy woman in an icy sleigh. She demanded to know who he was and what he was doing there. After Edmund gorged himself on Turkish Delight, the White Witch insisted that he must visit her at her castle, bringing along his brother and sisters.

Everyone agrees that Edmund followed the White Witch, but some believe that Edmund should have followed her and some believe that Edmund should not have followed her. Edmund should not have followed the White Witch for three reasons: Edmund purposely ignored a warning, carelessly overlooked the White Witch, and secretly followed Lucy into Narnia.

The first reason Edmund should not have followed the White Witch is that he purposely ignored a warning. The White Witch introduced herself to Edmund as "The Queen of Narnia," but Lucy, who had already met with real creatures in Narnia, called her the "White Witch." We know from fairy tales and literature that witches are evil. Therefore he should not have followed evil.

The second reason that Edmund should not have followed the White Witch is that he carelessly overlooked the White Witch. Initially, the White Witch was very cruel to Edmund, and his first instinct was to be scared of her. She fed him Turkish Delight only when she wanted to get something from him, like a fisherman feeds a worm on a hook to the fish he wants to catch and eat. Edmund, with his own eyes, should have seen from this interaction that the White Witch was evil.

The third reason Edmund should not have followed the White Witch is that he secretly followed Lucy into Narnia. From his very core, Edmund knew that he was doing wrong because he secretly left his siblings and the Beavers and did not discuss his plan with them. He could have been honest and open, but he chose to be deceitful and secretive—probably because they would have not gone along with his plan. Edmund knew that he was betraying his family and innocent creatures.

Some people say that Edmund should have followed the White Witch. They argue that the White Witch took care of Edmund, feeding him Turkish Delight and speaking kindly to him. However, this idea is invalid because we see the White Witch's true personality later. We see that she did not really care about Edmund, but that she simply wanted to take over Narnia. Feeding Edmund Turkish Delight and speaking kindly to him was just a means to reaching her evil goal.

In addition, people argue that Edmund should have followed the White Witch because he was alone and scared; thus he could not use proper judgment. This argument is also invalid because Edmund was not really alone. He had his trusted sister, Lucy, with him, and she had already testified that the White Witch was evil. We know that Edmund followed the White Witch out of pride and selfish ambition.

Neither of these arguments—that the White Witch took care of Edmund, and that Edmund was alone and scared—would give Edmund any reason to follow the White Witch.

Edmund should not have followed the White Witch because he purposely ignored a warning, carelessly overlooked the White Witch, and secretly followed Lucy into Narnia. Edmund **caused careless casualties** not only for himself, but—even worse—for his siblings and for all of Narnia.

SAMPLE ESSAY B

Imagine giving up your most precious possession. In the short story "The Gift of the Magi" by O. Henry, the main character was faced with this very decision.

Della and Jim, newlyweds living in New York City, are quickly finding out that married life is not without problems. Jim's salary has been reduced and their financial obligations have remained the same. In spite of her thrift and industry, Della finds herself on Christmas Eve with less than two dollars with which <u>to purchase a present for her precious</u> husband.

Everyone agrees that Della greatly desires to give a gift to her husband, Jim, for Christmas, however some feel Della should cut and sell her hair to pay for the gift while others feel Della should not cut and sell her hair.

Della should cut her hair for three reasons: to sacrifice, to show love, and to celebrate Christmas.

The first reason Della should cut her hair is to sacrifice. Her long hair is the most valuable possession she owns. Della derives great pleasure from catching a glimpse of herself in the small mirror in her flat. She feels like a queen and *her hair is her crown*. To cut her hair off will be a permanent decision. Her hair, most likely, will not grow back to that great length. She may not have much money, but she has a marketable commodity. By giving up her most precious possession, she will change her looks dramatically.

The second reason Della should cut her hair is to show love. In the throes of young love, this doting wife desires to show her husband the depth of her love for him. Throughout the story, the author pictures Jim as a caring provider, tenderly seeing to his wife. It makes perfect sense that Della would want to find a way to return that commitment with a gesture of her own.

The third reason Della should cut her hair is to celebrate Christmas. As the season of giving surrounds her, festive decorations and fancy shop windows remind Della of the approaching holiday. In a large city such as New York, advertisements, shop windows, and newspapers would all serve as reminders that while everyone else may be shopping for his special someone, Della has no means to do so. By cutting her hair she not only can give Jim a gift, but also a perfect complement to the family heirloom.

Some claim that Della should not sell her hair. After all, what might her husband's reaction be? Jim might not like her new hairstyle, might not approve of her sacrifice, and might hurt his career by having a wife who looks like a "Coney Island chorus girl." But there is no evidence to support this assertion. Della claims that a new watch chain might in fact help his standing in the community. A husband who would willingly sacrifice his own precious possession surely would not chastise his wife for selling hers.

In addition, some argue that the couple's budget is reason enough to put any spare change into savings. How can they justify such an impractical gift in the face of their present poverty? Jim wears a shabby coat, his salary has recently been reduced, and Della must bargain with the grocers for any savings she can. This reasoning is faulty. Even in the midst of less than ideal circumstances, a grand generous gesture can serve to remind us of the value of true love and sacrifice. Appropriate to the season of giving, Della can give.

Thus, neither Jim's potential reaction nor the couple's budget is enough to dissuade Della from selling her beautiful, valuable hair.

Della should sell her hair to sacrifice, show love, and celebrate Christmas. This matters to our friends, family, and members of our community as we all need a picture of what Christmas is all about. What matters is not the value of the gifts one receives, but of the gifts one gives.

GLOSSARY

Active voice: The verb form or voice in which the subject of the sentence performs or causes the action expressed by the verb.

Alliteration: A scheme involving the occurrence of the same letter or sound at the beginning of adjacent or closely connected words.

Amplification: Part of an essay's conclusion in which the writer states to whom his issue matters, and why it matters to that person or group.

Antecedent: An event that precedes another event, but does not necessarily cause it. We think about the antecedent when we apply the topic of Relation to the issue. "Ante" is from Latin, meaning "before." "Cede" is from Latin, meaning "to go."

Antithesis: A scheme in which strongly contrasting (or opposite) concepts are expressed in a parallel form.

Arrangement: The canon of composition by which the author orders the materials gathered in the Invention canon in a manner suited to the type of essay being written. It is sometimes called *dispositio*.

Arrangement Template: The pattern on which the outline is modeled; the structure of the essay in outline form.

Assonance: A rhetorical scheme in which a vowel sound is repeated in adjacent or closely connected words.

Common Topics: The Five Common Topics - Comparison, Definition, Circumstance, Relation, and Testimony – are places we go to gather information, from the Greek word, "topos," place.

Canon(s): The three fundamental activities of writing. They are Invention, Arrangement, and Elocution.

Cause: The actions, events, etc., that cause brought about the situation.

Circumstance: one of the Five Common Topics; Circumstance describes the actions and events that occur at the same time as, but in different locations from, the situation in which the issue arises.

Comparison: One of the Five Common Topics of Invention, Comparison asks how two terms (things, characters, places, ideas, etc.) are similar by noting what both terms "have", "are", and "do".

Conclusion: In writing, it is the ending of a text. It is prepared after the body of the text, and before the Introduction.

Consequent: An action that follows an event. This is part of the topic of Relation.

Counter-thesis: The statement of the position in direct opposition to the thesis

Definition: One of the five common topics. A definition of a word sets the limits within which a word has meaning. A definition of a thing identifies the genus and differentia of the thing defined. Definition asks the questions, "To what category does a thing belong?" "How does it compare to other members of that set?" and "What are its parts or aspects?" A formal definition states the genus (group) and differentia (unique qualities) of a term.

Differences of Degree: Differences of degree are expressed when one term is, has, or does more or less than other term. This is commonly expressed with the words more/less and better/worse.

Differences of Kind: Differences in kind are expressed when one term belongs to a different group then another term.

Differentiae: The differences between a term and the other members of its genus. In the topic of Definition, we ask what group (genus) our term belongs to, and how it is different from other members of the group.

Discovery: The first canon of rhetoric, during which the writer seeks and finds material for writing. This canon is also called Invention.

Disposition: The second canon of rhetoric, during which the writer sorts and arranges materials gather during Invention. This canon is also called Arrangement, or *dispositio*.

Distribution: The portion of the Division that states the thesis, enumeration, and exposition.

Division: A precise statement of the agreement and disagreement between the writer and an opponent.

Effect: The result of an action or cause.

Elocution: The third canon of rhetoric in which the writer selects the appropriate words and forms to best express the ideas of the text. This canon is also called Style.

Enumeration: A statement of the number of reasons you will use to support your thesis statement.

Essay Cycle: A complete set of teaching material for one essay that includes all three canons. This curriculum contains 10 lessons, with the first as an introduction. The 9 lessons in the middle will each take three weeks to teach.

Exercise: An action or series of actions by which the student practices the skill he is learning.

Exordium: The opening of an essay or speech, placed at the beginning of the introduction. Its purpose is to make the audience receptive to the speech or essay so they will listen.

Exposition: A statement of the main points in an essay or speech.

Genus: The category or group to which the thing defined belongs; the first part of a term's definition.

Idea: The universal concept that is abstracted out of individual types by a process of comparison. The meaning of an idea can never be exhausted.

Interesting Column: The column on the ANI chart used to record ideas generated during the Invention process that are not clearly Affirmative or Negative.

All the information students generate during Invention that does not belong to the "A" or "N" column should be considered part of the "I" column, even if they do not copy it onto the chart.

Introduction: The first part of an essay, developed after the body and the Conclusion of the essay are written.

Invention: The first canon of rhetoric during which the writer discovers material (an inventory) for the text. This canon is also called Discovery; coming up with something to say when we write.

Issue: A question converted to a whether statement. The Issue serves to generate questions about both the affirmative and negative responses to the question. Students generate a new issue for each new essay.

Lesson Guide: An independent lesson that teaches one tool or idea from the canon of which it is a part.

Metaphor: a trope, is an indirect comparison of two different kinds of things. (indirect- i.e. you do not use like or as).

Narratio: Narrative; also called a "statement of facts" or "statement of circumstances". It tells a story, with settings, actors, and actions, to inform the reader about the circumstances they need to know about the subject, or thesis, of the essay.

Parallelism: A similarity of structure in a pair or series of related words, phrases, or clauses (sentences).

Passive voice: a verb form or voice in which the grammatical subject receives the verb's action.

Part of speech: One of the traditional categories of words intended to reflect their grammatical functions of the words: nouns, pronouns, adjectives, verbs, adverbs, prepositions, interjections, and conjunctions.

Proof: This term has two uses in *The Lost Tools of Writing* ™: 1) The body of an essay; it contains the main arguments or reasons, with their supports, for the thesis. 2) The main reasons that make up the "proof" of the first sense. Each main reason includes three "sub-proofs."

Proposition: The judgment expressed by a statement. Its predicate affirms or denies something about its subject. It is either true or false.

Question: An interrogative sentence in which a speaker seeks information or confirmation. A question is the starting point of thought, and therefore, of each essay.

Reason: An argument or proof in defense of a thesis.

Refutation: The response to an opposing argument. For the persuasive essay, you anticipate two arguments that your opponent will have against your thesis. A refutation states those two counter-proofs and why they are inadequate.

Relation: one of the Five Common Topics; Relation lists events or actions that take place before and after the situation in which the issue arises and determines which are causes of the situation and which could be the effects of the actor's decisions (for or against).

Scheme: An arrangement of words or letters appealing to the senses (along with tropes, sometimes called "figures of speech"), e.g., a rhyme scheme.

Simile: Simile is a trope that makes an explicit comparison of two things different in kind but sharing a common characteristic. It uses words as "like" or "as" to make the comparison.

Situation: The Setting, Actors, and dilemma in which the Issue arises. The situation is developed much further in the lessons on Narratio and Relation.

Species: Other members of the group ("genus") that a term (in an issue) belongs to. In logic, these are specific things that are members of the genus, or group. We define specific terms from our issues

Style: Also called Elocution.

Summary: A brief statement of the totality of all the ideas presented. In a Persuasive Essay, the summary is in the conclusion. It includes the thesis and three main reasons.

Teacher: One who mediates an idea from his soul to the soul of a student.

Teaching: Mediating an idea from one soul to another.

Template: A pattern. The template is the form to imitate when we make an outline for our essays.

Terms: Word or expression used to name a thing.

Testimony: One of the five common topics; sometimes this topic is called Authority. Testimony asks witnesses what they know about the situation or event.

Thesis: The statement of the proposition defended by an essay. A thesis is derived from a question when the writer: 1) converts the question to an issue, 2) decides which side to defend, and 3) restates the issue as a statement representing the affirmative or negative position.

Topics: Question we ask in order to come up with something to say when we write.

Trope: An arrangement of words appealing to the mind or imagination (along with schemes, sometimes called "figures of speech"), e.g., a metaphor.

Type: An example or model from which something is made.

Universal: An idea or concept that is drawn out of (abstracted from) the particulars or types. For example, we learn "blue, red, yellow" as particulars, and then we understand the universal idea of "color." The universal is what all the particulars have in common.

Worksheet: In this curriculum, a worksheet is the form that guides the student or teacher through a pattern that they will learn to imitate. The goal of a worksheet is to help a person internalize a pattern of thinking so that the worksheet is no longer needed.

LESSON

SUMMARIES

ESSAY ONE

Invention: From Question to ANI

Essay One Invention teaches the first two steps for writing a persuasive essay:

1. Turn a question into an Issue.
2. Discover basic information by filling out the ANI chart.

To turn a question into an Issue, restate the question as a phrase that begins with the word "whether." For example, if your question is, "Should Edmund have followed the White Witch?" your Issue is, "Whether Edmund should have followed the White Witch." If your question is, "Was Achilles right to be angry with Agamemnon?" your Issue is, "Whether Achilles was right to be angry with Agamemnon."

The next step is to discover and organize information related to the Issue according to whether it argues for or against the issue, or whether it is argues for neither. To do this, complete the ANI chart (ANI stands for Affirmative, Negative, and Interesting). If a piece of information argues for the Affirmative, place it in the A column. If it argues for the Negative, place it in the N column. If it is simply an interesting fact, place it in the I column.

For example, if your issue is, "Whether Edmund should have followed the White Witch," in the A column, you might place bits of information like this: she gave him Turkish Delight, he didn't know she was a witch, he was cold and hungry, he was lost. In the N column, you might place information like this: Lucy had warned him about her, she wasn't kind to her horses or the dwarf, she yelled at Edmund, he would be sneaking away from his siblings. In the I column, place interesting pieces of information: the White Witch had a sled, it was winter, he and his siblings had been playing hide-and-go-seek, and she was very tall.

These first two steps - creating an issue out of a question and completing the ANI chart - lay the foundation for the persuasive essay.

Arrangement: From ANI to Outline

Essay One Arrangement introduces a number of names for the parts of an essay, including *Proof, Thesis, Introduction, Conclusion, Enumeration,* and *Exposition*. The *Thesis* is the statement that the essay defends. The *Proof* states the main reasons for the Thesis. If the Issue is, "Whether Edmund should have followed the White Witch," the Negative Thesis is, "Edmund should not have followed the White Witch." The Proof then lists three reasons that support the Negative position.

The *Introduction* is the opening to an essay and the *Conclusion* summarizes the essay by reviewing the argument. The *Enumeration* is the number of reasons the essay presents in support of its thesis and the *Exposition* presents the main points that make up the Proof.

Arrangement One presents an Arrangement Template that organizes these elements into a Rudimentary Persuasive Essay.. It lays a foundation on which ensuing essays grow.

Elocution: From Outline to Text
While the Student Workbook does *not* contain a worksheet for Elocution One, but you will learn to turn the outline from Arrangement One into a Rudimentary Persuasive Essay. You do this by making complete sentences out of the phrases and key words used in their outlines.
The first Rudimentary Persuasive Essay prioritizes structure, not eloquence. It initiates the discipline that the rest of the essays will demand. Do not worry about this essay sounding good, but about it being organized according to the proper structure.

ESSAY TWO

Invention: Introduction to the Five Topics
Essay Two briefly introduces the Five Topics of Invention. The Five Topics are tools for gathering information. The Topics are **Comparison**, **Definition**, **Circumstance**, **Relation**, and **Testimony**. Central to classical rhetoric, each of these five topics contains sub-questions that help the essay writer generate information pertaining to the issue.

The topic of **Comparison** asks, "How is X similar to Y?" and, "How is X different from Y?" For example, the writer might compare Edmund to Peter by asking how Edmund is similar to Peter. They are both brothers to Lucy and Susan, they are both British males, and they both go to Narnia. Also, both are characters in the book. However, they are different in that Peter is older, is less mean to Lucy, and does not sneak away from the group.
The topic of **Definition** asks, "Who or what is X?" and, "What kind of thing is X?" If X is Edmund, we might say that he is a boy from England who is in *The Lion, the Witch, and the Wardrobe*. We might also say that he is a brother and a son, that he becomes a king, and that he is a character in a book.

Circumstance asks, "What was happening at the time of the situation?" If we ask about the issue discussed above, we might ask, "What was happening in Narnia when Edmund met the White Witch?" and we might answer by recalling that Narnia was in the middle of a 100-year winter or that the White Witch was turning creatures into stone. We might also ask, "What was happening in England, Europe, or Calormen at that time?"

Relation asks what happened before and after the situation in which the issue arose. It is particularly interested in cause and effect. If we ask, "What happened immediately before and after Edmund followed the White Witch?" we might respond by recalling that Edmund and his siblings had been sent to stay with an older professor during the war and that they had been arguing about whether Lucy was just imagining Narnia. Afterward, we might note, they became kings and queens of Narnia.

Finally, **Testimony** asks, "What do witnesses say about the issue?" We might ask what Tumnus, a witness to the actions and character of the White Witch, can offer as testimony.

These topics and their accompanying questions are powerful tools to help the student complete an ANI chart and discover ideas. More significantly, they are universal, powerful tools for anybody who has a decision to make.

Arrangement A: A Guide To Sorting

In Essay Two Arrangement you will learn to sort and categorize the information on the ANI charts into groups by using symbols, such as @, $, or &. To do this, place a symbol of their choosing next to the first item in the affirmative and negative columns. Determine which items in each column might be organized into the same group as the first item. Place the same symbol next to all of the items that fit into this group. Follow the same process for every item in each column until every item has a corresponding symbol next to it. Each symbol thus corresponds to a group into which the items in the columns have been catalogued.

Next, choose an appropriate heading, or name, for each group. Then select three groups that have at least three members each. Those groups become the Proofs and the group members become the Sub-Proofs. Reviewing those Proofs, choose the side of the Issue - the Affirmative or the Negative – that you will defend.

Arrangement B: Introductory Persuasive Essay Outline. In Essay Two, you add Sub-Proofs to each of the three Proofs. Using the items sorted with Arrangement Worksheet A, fill out Worksheet B and its corresponding template to create a slightly more complicated outline than the Essay One version.

Elocution: Scheme – Parallelism 1: Words
Parallelism, a scheme, is a similarity of structure in a pair or series of related words, phrases, or clauses.

For example, when writers form a list in a sentence, each item in the list should be the same part of speech. When they combine phrases with a semi-colon, the grammatical structure of the two phrases should be identical.

Parallelism gives harmonious form, interest, and beauty to a sentence or passage. For example, consider the following correct usage of parallelism:

"Ronald Reagan was an actor, a governor, and a president."

On the other hand, consider the following non-parallel sentence (error in bold):

Ronald Reagan was an actor, a governor, ***and then he presided over the country.***

ESSAY THREE

Invention: Comparison - Similarities
Essay Three Invention introduces Comparison, one of the Common Topics. The topic of Comparison invites the student to discover similarities between two terms by examining what both terms **are, have, and do.**

For example, both Edmund and the White Witch are human-like beings, both have relationships, and both do harm to others.

Arrangement: A Guide to Exordium

Every essay should open with something to catch the reader's attention and set the tone for the rest of the essay. This opening is called the Exordium, and in Essay Three Arrangement you learn three types of Exordium: the **question**, the **challenge**, and the **quotation**. When used properly, each can pique the interest and attention of the reader before you have even presented your Thesis.

In an essay about whether Edmund should have followed the White Witch, you might ask a question like, "Have you ever been tempted by something that seemed too good to be true?" or "Have you ever been misled by someone who seemed good?"

You might challenge readers to never do anything wrong again or to do something as simple as "Listen!" or "Lend me your ears." Any imperative statement directed at the audience is a challenge to them. To begin with a quotation, you could present a text from the Bible on the dangers of pride or from a famous writer on the dangers of following leaders who buy your loyalty.

Elocution: Basic Editing - Verbs

This lesson focuses on two common verb problems: passive verbs and vague verbs. You should avoid them and replace them with more active and precise verbs. Passive verbs should be avoided because they tend to obscure the actor, while vague verbs communicate less meaning than more precise verbs.

A passive verb is a verb in which the subject of the sentence is not acting but is being acted upon. For example, in the sentence, "The book was lost by the man," the subject - the book - is not acting, but is being acted upon. It would usually be better to say, "The man lost the book."

Vague verbs lack specificity, so they are common, like *are, do, have, got, went, etc.* as in, "He got himself closer to the window." Sometimes, vague verbs are aided by helping verbs, as in "Ickey does a dance." It would usually be better to say, "Ickey dances," or "He drew closer to the window," or even, "He approached the window." Do a hunt for unnecessary helping verbs and get overly common verbs and you'll find plenty of vague verbs to replace.

Strong verbs are the life-blood of a sentence. Without vigorous, energetic, specific verbs, a sentence struggles to express the writer's ideas.

ESSAY FOUR

Invention: Comparison - Degree and Kind

As you learned in Essay Three, you can compare any two items by looking for their similarities: asking what both terms are, have, and do. In Essay Four Invention, you compare terms to find differences.

Things can differ in two ways: one can be, have, or do more or less than the other, or one can be, have, or do a different kind of thing from the other. The first is a difference of degree, the second a difference of kind.

The most obvious way to find differences is simply to ask how the terms are different and to note the differences identified. That is a good place to start. But in this lesson, you learn to refine the search.

To find Comparisons of Degree and Kind, first, find similarities between two terms, as you did in Comparison One. Then draw differences of degree or kind from the similarities.

For instance, a pen and a pencil are both writing instruments. To find a difference of degree, ask which one is better and why or which one has more of something than the other (such as length) and by how much. Of course, the normal way to ask the second question is to ask which is longer, a difference of degree.

Both Edmund and the White Witch are living beings. To find a difference in kind, ask what kind of living being Edmund is (human boy) and then ask what kind of living being the White Witch is (purportedly a half jinn-half giant woman).

Arrangement: A Guide to Amplification

Amplification is a concluding statement that answers the questions, *Who cares?* and, *Why?* To write an Amplification, first identify the audience to whom the essay or speech is addressed. Then identify a group about whom that audience cares and how the decision might affect them.

The audience could be the writer's friends, Mr. Tumnus, or even the teacher. Groups the audience cares about could be family, the Narnians, or the teacher's students. The decision could affect these groups in various ways, among them: the Narnians could be permanently subjected to the White Witch if Edmund follows her and betray his siblings. It is for the writer to determine which audience to address, which group that audience cares about, and how the decision might affect them.

ESSAY FIVE

Invention: Definition I

Essay Five focuses on the Topic of Definition. You define a thing or idea by identifying the group it belongs to and how it is different from all the other members of that group.

For each essay, you will define one or more terms from your issue. A *term* is a word or phrase that names a particular thing (a person, idea, place, emotion, etc.) or a particular action. If you are writing about the issue, "Whether Edmund should have followed the White Witch," your terms are the words *Edmund, followed, and White Witch*. Words like articles and helping verbs are technically terms as well, but you do not need to define them.

To define the term *Edmund:*

-Identify what kind of thing *Edmund* is. What is he? He is a boy, a citizen of Great Britain, a brother and son, and a character in a book.

-Decide which of these groups will be most helpful as you think about the term in the context of this essay. For the sake of simplicity, let's choose *boys* as the group to examine.

-Identify other members of the group *boys,* such as Peter (Edmund's brother), Tom Sawyer, Dennis the Menace, Harry Potter, or Charlie Brown.

-Consider why each member of the list above is a member of the group *boys.* Identify properties or characteristics they all share. So we might identify them as older than babies but younger than men.

-Identify characteristics that make the term *Edmund* different from every other member of the group *boys.* These characteristics are called *differentia,* and the writer needs them to differentiate this Edmund from any others. We might say that Edmund was a character in this particular book that he was Peter's younger brother, that he was a king of Narnia, or that he was motivated by envy.

To write the definition for the term *Edmund,* we include only the term, its group, and its necessary differences. *Edmund is a boy, the younger brother of Peter Pevensie, motivated by envy.*

Arrangement: A Guide to Division

Division identifies the point of disagreement between the writer and those who hold the opposing view. The purpose of the Division is to clarify the agreement and to specify the exact point of disagreement. After all, it is useless – and all too common - to debate a point upon which both sides agree.

To create the Division, follow these steps:

- Write the Thesis.
- Write the Counter-Thesis (the opposing position).
- Compare the two statements and determine areas where the sides agree.

For example, in an essay about whether Edmund should have followed the White Witch, the Thesis for the Negative would be, "Edmund should not have followed the White Witch," while the Counter-Thesis would be, "Edmund should have followed the White Witch." After comparing the two theses, you might note (with help from the Essay Five Arrangement student worksheet) that both sides agree that Edmund, did, in fact, follow her. The point of contention, however, is whether he should have.

Unless an essay or discussion clearly articulates where the Division lies (and with it the common ground) it runs the risk of arguing in circles, harming relationships, and failing to resolve real issues.

Elocution : Antithesis

Antithesis is a scheme that arranges contrasting ideas in adjacent clauses that follow the same grammatical pattern. Create Antithesis by asserting a clause, inserting a contrasting conjunction (such as *but*) or (for writers who understand them) a semi-colon, and asserting a second clause that strongly contrasts with the first. Consider the following examples:

- *I'd rather be dirt poor and loved than filthy rich and despised.*
- *Woe to you who laugh now, for you will mourn and weep.*
- *Not that I loved Caesar less, but that I loved Rome more.*

To add Antithesis to the essay, identify a sentence or passage that contrasts two or more things (such as Edmund and Peter, Edmund and the White Witch, etc.) and then rewrite the sentence using a parallel structure that emphasizes the contrast. You might want to write, "Peter was a responsible leader but Edmund was an impudent loner," or, "Edmund was cold, hungry and afraid, while the White Witch was warm, fed, and powerful."

Antithesis is a powerful tool for emphasizing the differences between terms and ideas.

ESSAY SIX

Invention: Circumstance
The Topic of Circumstance helps you discover information about your issue by asking what was happening at *the time* of the issue. First, ask what was happening in the situation where the issue arose, then move outward to various locations surrounding the situation.

If you are thinking about whether Edmund should have followed the White Witch, ask what was happening around him when Edmund stumbled upon the White Witch. You can even begin by asking what was happening in Edmund's or the White Witch's mind.

Next, ask what was happening elsewhere in Narnia at the time, or what was happening at the Professor's house, or in London. You are not concerned at this point whether the events are related to the issue; that comes in the next lesson.

Arrangement: A Guide to Refutation
A Refutation is a response to a counter-argument. When you write a Persuasive Essay, you affirm your Thesis by presenting Proofs that support your position. But not everyone will agree, and those who don't will choose the opposing position. In the Refutation, you describe the opposing position and then state why that position is inadequate.

For example, while you might argue that Edmund should not have followed the White Witch, someone else might argue that he should have. In your Refutation, you list your opponents best reasons (e.g. he was lonely, cold, and hungry) and then you explain why those reasons are insufficient (e.g. they only consider the short term).

To write a Refutation, follow these steps. First, state the Counter-Thesis. This is the statement that opposes your Thesis. Second, choose two of the strongest reasons that support the Counter-Thesis. You have already discovered and sorted the material for these reasons in your ANI, so return to your sorted ANI and select two Proofs from the A or N column. Remember, this will be the position *you did not choose to defend*. Third, list three supports for each Counter-Thesis Proof. Fourth explain why these reasons are not compelling enough. Finally, briefly summarize your Refutation.

Elocution: Simile
A simile is a trope that makes an explicit comparison of two things different in kind but sharing a striking quality. Similes use such comparison words as *like* or *as* to make the comparison explicit.

To write a simile, follow three steps. First, select something in your sentence that you want to emphasize (usually because it has a quality you want to draw out). Second, list some of its characteristics or qualities and select one to highlight. Third, link the first thing to a different kind of thing that shares a similar characteristic or quality by using a comparison word, such as *like* or *as*.

For instance, if you want to emphasize the White Witch, start by listing some of her characteristics and qualities. You might note that she is deceptive. Next, name a different kind of thing that is also deceptive and link the White Witch to that thing with a comparison word. For example, a fisherman deceives to catch a fish. Your simile is, "The White Witch used Turkish Delight to catch Edmund like a fisherman uses bait to catch a fish."

ESSAY SEVEN

Invention: Relation

Using the Topic of Relation, you gather information by listing the events or actions that took place before the situation and those that followed the actor's decision. Next, review the list of preceding actions and events to identify which might be causes of the situation. Finally, review the list of actions and events that followed the decision to identify which are effects (i.e. are caused by the decision made).

Some essays may look at the Issue assuming that the decision is not yet made. In that case, writers should list possible or probable effects of the affirmative and negative decisions.

For the issue, "Whether Edmund should have followed the White Witch," begin by asking what happened (actions and events) before Edmund met the White Witch. Then ask what happened after Edmund decided to follow the White Witch.

Next, select the actions or events that caused Edmund to be in the situation (confronted by the White Witch in Narnia), and the actions or events caused or probably caused by the decision (effects).

To find actions or events that caused the situation, ask, "What caused the actor to be in this situation?" To find actions or events that the decision caused, ask, "What happened because of the decision made?"

If you assume that Edmund has not yet made his decision, you would ask, "What will likely happen if Edmund does follow the White Witch? What if he doesn't?" This is frequently an excellent perspective to take when students are in the middle of a story or when you are leading a discussion.

Arrangement: A Guide to Narratio

The Narratio is a simple narration of background information that helps the reader understand the context of your thesis. The Narratio is placed before the Thesis in the Template.

The Narratio consists of the situation (time, place, characters), and the events or actions (the causes) that led to the situation. Thus, the Invention lesson on the Topic of Relation prepares students for this lesson.

To write a Narratio, follow these four steps:

- Describe the situation of the issue.

- Generate a list of actions or events that led to the situation by asking, "How did the actor get in this situation? What caused this situation?"

- Ask, "And what caused that cause?"

- Convert this chain of causes into a simple narration.

If you argue that Edmund should not have followed the White Witch, generate a Narratio by asking, "When and where did this take place?" and, "Who was involved?" Edmund is in the White Witch's sleigh during the 100 year Narnian winter.

Then ask, "How did the actor get there?" He walked through a wardrobe. "And what caused that?" He was playing hide and seek with his siblings. "And how did that happen?" They needed something to do while at the Professor's house in the country because of the war.

Elocution: Alliteration

Alliteration is the repetition of initial *consonant* sounds in a phrase or verse. You are perhaps most familiar with the use of alliteration in tongue twisters like, "Peter Piper picked a peck of pickled peppers." Alliteration also gives titles a pleasing rhythm, such as *The Merry Wives of Windsor* or *The Lion, the Witch, and the Wardrobe.* But don't limit the value of alliteration (or assonance, see Essay Nine below) to tongue twisters and titles. Robert Louis Stevenson, one of the finest stylists in the English language, wrote: "The beauty of the contents of a phrase, or of a sentence, depends implicitly upon alliteration and upon assonance. You may follow the adventures of a letter through any passage that has particularly pleased you."

To add alliteration, follow these steps. First, identify a word, phrase, or clause that you want to emphasize or improve with a better sound. Second, identify a consonant sound that you want to repeat. Third, generate a list of words that contain the same consonant sound, and, finally, select several words from the list that fit and add them to your original sentence.

For instance, consider the following sentence, "The White Witch made Narnia a total mess." You might wish to repeat the "w" sounds found in white and witch. You could change the words *total mess* to *wasteland,* and replace the word *made* with *wielded her power.* The new sentence will read, "The White Witch wielded her power and turned Narnia into a wasteland."

ESSAY EIGHT

Invention: Testimony—Witnesses

You will learn to collect testimony (i.e. information) from witnesses. Witnesses can provide two kinds of testimony: direct observation of an action or event within the situation, or an actor's patterns of behavior that extend beyond the situation. Briefly, witness testimony provides firsthand knowledge of an action or of an actor's character.

To collect testimony from witnesses, follow four steps. First, identify witnesses to the situation. Second, list the actions or events they witnessed in the situation. Third, describe patterns of behavior they have witnessed in an actor beyond the situation. Finally, assess the reliability of the witness.

If your issue is, "Whether Edmund should have followed the White Witch," first, identify a witness to the situation, such as the dwarf. Then ask what he saw the White Witch or Edmund do in the situation. He could say that he saw the White Witch make Turkish Delight and put her warm robes around Edmund. Third, ask what patterns he has seen in her behavior. He has seen the White Witch lose her temper on many occasions, turning Narnians into stone. Finally, assess the dwarf's reliability. He is probably not a reliable witness because he is afraid of the White Witch.

You should feel free to use a new witness for the third step if, as is common, the first witness saw the situation, but has not seen the actor in other contexts.

Arrangement: Review
No new content is introduced in this review lesson.

Elocution: Metaphor
A metaphor compares two different kinds of things and draws a striking, implicit comparison. Unlike simile, metaphors avoid using comparison words such as *like or as*, and instead state that one object *is* the other object. In this way, metaphors make an indirect comparison between two things that are different in kind.

To create a metaphor, follow three steps. First, select a thing you want to describe with a metaphor. Second, list one of its characteristics or qualities. Third, think of another thing that shares that quality but is a different kind of thing from the first.

If you want to emphasize the White Witch, you could list some of her characteristics and qualities, like that she is controlling. Next, name a different kind of thing that is also controlling and directly link the White Witch to this object. A puppeteer is controlling, so you might write, "The White Witch is a puppeteer who controls all of Narnia."

ESSAY NINE

Elocution: Assonance
Similar to alliteration, assonance is the repetition of *vowel* sounds in a phrase or verse that emphasizes a key idea or adds a pleasant tone to your sentences. It is generally less obtrusive than alliteration, so it is more artistic and adaptable.

To generate assonance, choose words with similar internal vowel sounds and ground them near each other. For example: "Rage, rage against the **dying** of the **light**" (long "i" sound) and, "Wisely and slow, they **stumble** that **run** fast" (short "u" sound).

To add assonance, follow these steps. First, identify a word, phrase, or clause that you want to emphasize or give a better sound. Second, identify a vowel sound that you want to repeat. Third, generate a list of words that contain the same vowel sound, and, finally, select several from the list that fit and add them to your original sentence.

For instance, to improve the sentence, "Edmund was a selfish brother who betrayed his family for a piece of candy," you could focus on the strong verb "betrayed" and its long *A* sound. By changing *selfish* to *crave* and *piece* to *taste,* you create the following sentence: "Edmund was a power-craving brother who betrayed his family for a taste of candy." The new words make use of the long *A* sound and the sentence sounds at least a little better.

As with all Level One skills, assonance takes time to master. Give your students that time to practice and to use these many tools simply and even badly before you expect them to use them like master artists!